LOOSE PARTS FOR CHILDREN WITH DIVERSE ABILITIES

MIRIAM BELOGLOVSKY

Other Redleaf Press books by Miriam Beloglovsky and Lisa Daly

Loose Parts: Inspiring Play in Young Children
Loose Parts 2: Inspiring Play with Infants and Toddlers
Loose Parts 3: Inspiring Culturally Sustainable Environments
Loose Parts 4: Inspiring 21st Century Learning
Early Learning Theories Made Visible

Other Redleaf Press books by Miriam Beloglovsky and Michelle Grant-Groves

*Design in Mind: A Framework for Sparking Ideas, Collaboration,
    and Innovation in Early Education*

Loose Parts
for Children
with Diverse
Abilities

Miriam Beloglovsky

Redleaf Press®
www.redleafpress.org
800-423-8309

Published by Redleaf Press
10 Yorkton Court
St. Paul, MN 55117
www.redleafpress.org

First edition 2022
Cover design by Renee Hammes
Cover photographs by Miriam Beloglovsky
Interior design by Erin Kirk
Typeset in Berkeley Oldstyle and Trade Gothic
Printed in the United States of America
29 28 27 26 25 24 23 22   1 2 3 4 5 6 7 8

Library of Congress Cataloging-in-Publication Data

Names: Beloglovsky, Miriam, author.
Title: Loose parts for children with diverse abilities / by Miriam
    Beloglovsky.
Description: First edition. | St. Paul, MN : Redleaf Press, 2022. |
    Includes bibliographical references. | Summary: "Award-winning author
    and educator Miriam Beloglovsky advocates for play for play sake and
    invites early childhood educators and families to see children with
    diverse abilities' strengths, recognize them as capable, competent and
    creative, and listen to their powerful voices. This book addresses the
    importance of play while providing appropriate accommodation to support
    young children with diverse abilities"— Provided by publisher.
Identifiers: LCCN 2021054556 (print) | LCCN 2021054557 (ebook) |
    ISBN 9781605547077 (paperback) | ISBN 9781605547084 (ebook)
Subjects: LCSH: Play. | Early childhood education—Activity programs. |
    Children with disabilities—Education (Early childhood) | Creative
    activities and seat work. | Inclusive education.
Classification: LCC LB1139.35.P55 B46 2022 (print) | LCC LB1139.35.P55
    (ebook) | DDC 371.9/0472—dc23/eng/20220209
LC record available at https://lccn.loc.gov/2021054556
LC ebook record available at https://lccn.loc.gov/2021054557

Printed on acid-free paper

I dedicate this book to all educators who

- see children's strengths and unique ways of being in the world;

- have the courage to design inclusive and equitable early childhood ecosystems;

- create places of belonging where children with diverse abilities are valued as contributing members of the community;

- advocate for children's right to play; and

- believe in play, creativity, and innovation as components of quality and engagement.

Contents

Acknowledgments

This book was transformational for me. It is the first book that I have written on my own. It represents my values and beliefs, and I hope it demonstrates my passion for equity and inclusion. Writing a book independently does not mean that you don't have a strong team supporting you. I am fortunate to have a strong network of friends to walk with me through moments of doubt and concerns. This book represents how we can overcome complex challenges with support and trust. Notably, I wrote this book in the middle of a global pandemic and with limited access to early childhood programs where I could photograph. Thankfully, once again, friends, mentors, and colleagues opened the door to help me.

I want to thank Debbie McMannis and Casey Johnson of Lincoln Community Preschool in Lincoln, California (www.lincolncommunitypreschool.com), for their generosity and support. They opened their doors so I could photograph their program during COVID-19. They graciously shared stories and served as reflective partners during the writing of this book.

To Diane Spahn and Kasey Kile of Kodo Kids (https://kodokids.com), who generously took the time to take photographs, share stories, and help curate Loose Parts. Their dedication and commitment to children helped highlight the important points covered in this book.

To Rachel Marks, who helped me organize, photograph, and review the accommodations covered in the book. Her knowledge of children and occupational therapy was helpful as we chose Loose Parts and analyzed the provisions needed to infuse them into early childhood ecosystems.

I want to acknowledge the advisory council members. They took the time to serve as advisers and provided me valuable advice and ideas to consider as guidance to the writing of this book. Specifically, Michelle Grant-Groves guided the process and served as a mentor and advocate. The book is better because of you.

I know this probably is cliché, but I want to extend a big shout-out to my editor, Melissa York. She kept me organized, and her ability to see beyond the words and read between the lines made the book stronger. Her encouragement and patience truly helped me make decisions and learn to trust my writing.

I am thankful for my daughter Alexis Baran's willingness to photograph Loose Parts despite her busy schedule. Your artistic and design capacities never cease to amaze me.

I want to recognize my daughter Arielle Baran, who always reminds me to see the positive side of life and to keep advocating for my beliefs. She is an inspiration, and I admire and aspire to follow her commitment to social justice.

I can't forget all the friends who helped me collect Loose Parts and who kindly shared their unexpected discoveries with me. I could not succeed without your support, encouragement, and commitment to make me a better writer and educator. Esther Villa, Michael Leeman, Chris Marks, Jacob Marks, Megan Matteoni, and Maurice Sykes (who keeps me true to my beliefs)—and many others who have supported me through the years—I love you and thank you!

LOOSE PARTS FOR CHILDREN
WITH DIVERSE ABILITIES

Chapter 1
The Importance of Inclusive Ecosystems and Loose Parts

Gears, twigs, leaves— little children love the world. That is why they are so good at learning about it. For it is love, not tricks and techniques of thought, that lies at the heart of all true learning. Can we bring ourselves to let children learn and grow through that love?—John Holt

It is not news that children have an innate need to play. Play is a magnificent activity that sustains life and promotes joy and hopefulness. Play appears at any age, at any stage, and throughout human history in every geographical area and every culture. Children make meaning of their world through play. They benefit from child-initiated and child-directed play opportunities. Children with diverse abilities or special rights also have an innate desire to play and engage in self-sustained play. Therefore play is a crucial right for children with diverse abilities, and it must be respected, nurtured, and encouraged.

This book addresses the importance of play while providing appropriate accommodations to support young children with diverse abilities. We must appreciate play for the sake of play and not as a medium to obtain educational goals or promote the development of children with diverse abilities. I write this book as a commitment and an invitation to early childhood educators and families to see children with diverse abilities' strengths, to recognize them as capable, competent, and creative, and to listen to their powerful voices. I invite you to create ecosystems based on the practices of peace and freedom where children can become valued members of the community. Together we must work toward changing the current educational narrative that silences the voices of many children, and too often, those of children with diverse abilities.

As a society, we can't remain passive and compliant with the current educational system, which focuses on meeting standards rather than creating citizens of the world. We must join hands and work toward creating ecosystems—biological communities of interacting organisms and their physical environments—where every community member is valued and supported. Places where we hear every voice because we are committed to education that serves liberation and freedom rather than promoting oppression and minimizing people by reducing them to a label or an assumption based on negative perspectives.

As I write this book, we are experiencing an incredibly devastating COVID-19 pandemic that has shed light on many inequalities existing in this country. At the same time, we see the emergence of the Black Lives Matter movement's united voices, which has ignited a new push for social justice. It is becoming harder and harder for society to look away from the many inequities occurring in communities of color and communities that face economic disadvantages. Families living with food insecurity, homelessness, or excessive economic disadvantages, including a lack of health care, have been more vulnerable to the pandemic's effects. In many instances, these are the same families that have experienced the mistreatment and violence of governmental authorities and educational systems. Rooted in Eurocentric practices, these systems separate children into categories that determine their success and failure—thus supporting ongoing and systemic racism, classism, and ableism. The impact is magnified for children with diverse abilities.

Throughout this time, I have engaged in conversations with many educators and families about the impact of online learning and physical distancing. We feel a collective concern that children with diverse abilities are not receiving the support and services they need. The circumstances and the need for physical distance moved children's learning to a virtual space—perhaps with little consideration for the many children who could not participate due to limitations that do not promote learning in a virtual format. That is why infusing play with Loose Parts as children have transitioned online is crucial to ensure that they continue to find joy and an intrinsic love for learning.

With play under attack by a culture steeped in excessive technology and constant pressure to meet academic standards (which do not reward creativity and playfulness), we risk losing the flexibility and adaptability that is achieved through play. There is a need for more research to deepen our knowledge and understanding of the influence of play on children with diverse abilities. However, we can continue to work with the assumption that play is crucial to the development of all children, and we must create inclusive ecosystems to support the play of children with diverse abilities. Shifting the language from the term *environments* to *ecosystems* allows us to see that every person, every object, and the design of the space are interconnected and affect one another. In an inclusive ecosystem, children are not only present but are considered active and valuable members of the family, school, and community. When we approach education from an ecosystem perspective, we begin to value beauty in humans and their surroundings as a catalyst for transforming children's lives.

In this book, I represent inclusion as the right children have to actively and fully participate in an educational ecosystem with all their gifts and capacities. Even when a disability is an integral part of who they are, it does not alone define them. As educators, we must create and design play ecosystems that support children regardless of their ability, race, ethnicity, socioeconomic status, language, family culture, or history. Educators can use a variety of adaptations to increase the participation of children with diverse abilities in the classroom ecosystem.

To create ecosystems of hope where creativity and innovation emerge, we have to use a play equity lens in all our practices. We must embrace the ethos that all children have the right to play and that no other adult agenda will replace this basic right. Often in education our focus is on meeting standards and assessing children for progress on an educational and developmental scale. We tend to forget that play brings joy and pleasure to people. Without joy and happiness, learning will not happen. The power of play equity is reflected in the following story.

Twins Brian and Bridget were born prematurely. They received early intervention services from birth. Bridget progressed faster than Brian, who had no mobility on his left side. He was protective of his left arm and refused to use it or allow people to touch it. When the twins entered an inclusive preschool, Bridget easily adjusted and enjoyed the sensory explorations and daily interactions with peers. Brian took longer to adjust but progressed steadily. Every morning Brian gravitated toward the shelf with natural Loose Parts and a basket of feathers. Brian enjoyed arranging and rearranging feathers in different configurations. He picked up one feather at a time and ran it up and down his left arm and hand. Little by little, he gained interest in other Loose Parts and learned to sit next to other children. One day Brian took one of the feathers and ran it up and down Silvie's arm. She quietly sat and allowed Brian to continue. After a few minutes, Silvie started laughing and turned to Brian, saying, "That tickles." Brian quietly extended his right arm so that Silvie could run the feather up and down. The Loose Parts served as a catalyst to include others in play and help them successfully socialize. Later the educators found out that the occupational therapist would gently move

soft objects up and down Brian's left arm to help him accept people gently touching it. Using this information, the educators decided to add more soft Loose Parts into the ecosystem for Brian to explore. They brought soft fabrics and ribbons for him to insert into tissue boxes. Observing and listening to children and taking the time to analyze what we observe is a valuable tool when creating inclusive ecosystems and filling them with Loose Parts.

The Language of Loose Parts

Loose Parts are materials that entice children of all abilities to explore and engage in sustainable play. We all have memories of playing with rocks, sticks, shells, and other natural or found materials. I remember collecting interesting metal bottle caps and playing intricate games with them. Loose Parts are inexpensive, or, even more often, free. They support children's interest in discovery and exploration, and they give full rein to children's imagination, creativity, and innovation. Loose Parts support educators in creating spaces where creative and joyful expression is inspired and where relationships are built through the sharing of ideas and interests. Loose Parts are non-prescriptive and can be used flexibly. This can be particularly helpful for children with diverse abilities, who manipulate the Loose Parts according to their abilities. Unlike toys, Loose Parts do not come with a predetermined set of directions that measure children's skills, knowledge, or capabilities. There is no right or wrong way to manipulate and use Loose Parts, so they diminish the possibility for failure and decrease anxiety and frustration. Loose Parts remind us that our focus needs to be on children's joy of play rather than assessing skills and striving for mastery.

The educational philosophy of Loose Parts provides children a language to express their ideas, feelings, and interests. The following are some examples of how Loose Parts enhance children's creative language:

- Loose Parts help children express who they are and how they perceive themselves.
- They support children in making connections and building relationships.
- They invite children to participate in something bigger than themselves.
- Beautiful Loose Parts invite children to look closely, notice details, and think about how they will use them to express their ideas.
- They support perspective-taking and gaining new understandings about themselves and the world.
- They offer multiple possibilities to explore and experiment.
- They promote innovation, creativity, and invention. They trigger that deep place that helps us say, "I have an idea."

- They offer educators a window into children's thinking and their perception of the world.
- They support children in expressing their emotions and feelings.
- They help adults express and extend children's ideas.
- They celebrate mistakes as opportunities to learn.
- They invite children and adults to collaborate.

Exploring Loose Parts requires educators to take a risk and suspend their previous conceptions of how children learn. Educators must play with Loose Parts, explore them, and create with them until the materials feel less risky and their value becomes clear. I invite you, the reader, to find yourself feeling inspired or curious about your discoveries.

Loose Parts to Inspire Adults to Be Joyful and Creative

Loose Parts can help families and educators recapture the joy of playing. It is challenging and exhausting to continually care for and educate children with diverse abilities. Families may feel tired of constantly worrying about their children. Educators may feel tired of creating adaptations to meet an Individualized Family Service Plan (IFSP) or Individualized Educational Plan (IEP). It is not surprising that educators and family members rely on store-bought toys that are promoted to help achieve specific skills. I want to invite educators and families to shift their perspective and consider the magic of Loose Parts to build the same skills and more.

Loose Parts are more than just objects that provide play opportunities. They are part of a powerful educational philosophy that supports playful inquiry and profound learning. I find that they bring hope and create a space for communication with children, educators, and families. One of the most amazing and creative endeavors for adults is finding Loose Parts and considering all the affordances or properties they offer children. Even before I began writing this book, reflecting on and, most important, playing with the different Loose Parts allowed me to consider the many possibilities. It also required me to look in many places, including nature, thrift shops, repurpose stores, and garage sales, where finding unexpected discoveries brought joy and appreciation for both recyclable and upcycled materials.

Everywhere I go I look for Loose Parts that can be infused into inclusive and equitable ecosystems. On a sojourn to my mother's hometown in Texas, I visited an antique shop and walked up and down the aisles, marveling at the different objects. The space once housed the five-and-dime variety retail store. The smell and the sound of the wooden floor brought back my childhood and how excited I felt when I could select a toy to take home. I looked and explored, touched,

and felt different objects. I pondered and wondered with deep curiosity. I finally stopped in front of a glass jar filled with handmade scrubbers used to wash dishes. I ran the scrubbers up and down my arm and manipulated them close to my ear to hear their sound. They were colorful and beautiful and would provide a wonderful textural exploration for young children. Joyfully I purchased thirty of them. On a visit to another antique shop, I was attracted to the history and possibilities of old doorknobs. I purchased them thinking that children with diverse abilities would enjoy exploring them and weighing them on my antique scale. Personally, I love the idea of including old objects in the early childhood ecosystem, as I believe they connect us to our past and our history and help bridge old and new technology while providing for a hopeful future.

With this book, I want to invite educators and families who joyfully support children with diverse abilities to encounter their own creativity as they find Loose Parts to engage children in play. Look through your own home—find your old buttons, and then sit with them and explore their colors, textures, sounds, and smells. Think, "How will children with diverse abilities explore them?" Search for fabrics that have beautiful patterns or pile up small towels with a variety of textures. Open a drawer and play with plastic storage containers. Stack and fold silicone cupcake holders, find silicone brushes to run through your fingers, or make dynamic sounds as you bang on pots and pans. Take a walk in nature and discover all the

beautiful gifts the earth gives us. My dear friend Michelle recently sent me a bag of amazing rose pine cones that her educator Jacky collected for me. I cherish them, and I know they will engage children to touch and explore them. Their spiral shape is also intriguing and reminds me of change and transformation.

Inspiration can be found in different places, from a visit to a friend's house (yes, I have been known to ask friends to give me napkin rings and other objects they no longer use), to a walk in the forest, a garage sale, or even your own cabinets. We just need to look at objects with a different lens—a lens that brings hope, intention, and understanding of both our interests as adults and the interests of children with diverse abilities.

Loose Parts Play for Children with Diverse Abilities

Play is that active, joyful way children choose to spend their time when they are not directed by adults. It is also the way that children, regardless of their ability or background, connect with one another. For example, Simone, who exhibits neurodiversity, finds playful ways to invite other children to play with her. On one occasion, Simone closely observes Jayme and Charlotte setting a table with cups, saucers, and small, colorful wood beads for a tea party. She approaches the space and touches Jayme's shoulder, smiles, and points to herself. Charlotte approaches Simone and says, "Yes, Simone, you can come to our tea party and taste the macaroons." Simone has developed a system of communication that other children understand. As the tea party continues, Simone takes some wooden chips and puts them on a plate. She points to them, picks one up, and brings her "macaroon" to

her mouth, pretending to eat it. Jayme says, "Thank you for the delicious cookies." For Simone, communication happens through body language—she is incredibly skilled when she engages in play that is meaningful to her.

When children play, they inhabit the fertile world between actuality and possibility. They incorporate what may be part of their imagination—such as being a fairy that changes people's lives—and combine it with real Loose Parts in the environment, creating fantasy lands that grow and change to accommodate their ideas. This is the creative process. Children with diverse abilities may hold on to this playfulness for a longer time than other children, and it must be regarded as a mark of strength, not disability. For children with diverse abilities, Loose Parts provide opportunities for children to do the following:

- test their abilities safely and bravely and gain confidence in their capacities
- fully participate in the classroom community and family life, feeling less isolated and more engaged
- understand how their bodies move and how they work
- engage in active learning and joyful and imaginative play
- explore and express emotions and feelings
- collaborate and co-construct knowledge with other children and adults
- heal, grow, communicate, and learn
- be energized, renewed, and inspired

With this book, I want to invite educators and families to more intentionally consider the tools and materials they offer children, incorporating, designing, and adapting Loose Parts to ensure successful outcomes for children with diverse abilities while continuing to build the empathy of children who are developing typically. We also hope to guide educators and families to successfully design spaces where belonging is central to learning and growing. I want to help educators and families deepen their understanding of how Loose Parts serve as a vehicle for children to express their thinking and knowledge of the world.

Because Loose Parts are open-ended and free of biases and stereotypes, they let children focus on strengths instead of deficits, and because Loose Parts support individual abilities and interests, they provide a way of looking at differences that connects rather than separates people. As children manipulate Loose Parts, they engage in thinking about themselves, the world, and the realities of other children. Adults can learn from the way children welcome learning, from their capacity to accept people who are different from them, and from their dedication to honoring others' unique qualities. For example, Aurelio spends most of his day in the construction space using almost every block and Loose Part to create complex structures. When other children join him, he recognizes that not everyone has the same building abilities, and he guides them to work on parts of his structure that require less precision.

We also want to discuss possible adaptations to make the Loose Parts even more inclusive. For example, when children are hospitalized and need to be in a sterile environment, what changes must families and educators make to ensure that the Loose Parts meet the hygiene and safety standards of the hospital setting? In addition, adapting Loose Parts can support the specific challenges children with diverse abilities may have. For example:

Physical limitations and/or restricted movement: Children who experience physical limitations or have restricted movement may need more space to maneuver a wheelchair or walker to access the Loose Parts. Educators can reposition shelves and organize the Loose Parts in containers that are easier to hold and transport. Trays and frames can contain the Loose Parts for easier reach and interaction. Children may be more successful in manipulating large objects or may need adaptive equipment to play with smaller Loose Parts. For example, Thomas, a preschooler who struggles with mobility, enters the outdoor space using a walker and finds large tree stumps (log sections) placed up against a fence. He holds on to the fence as he pulls himself up onto the first stump. He continues to hold on to the fence and cautiously walks from stump to stump. He does this for days, and the more he gains strength, the more skilled at walking he becomes. Soon Thomas starts joining other children as they plan games that incorporate the tree stumps. The hope of the educators and the family is that he will be able to walk without a walker and continue to participate in collaborative play.

Cognitive challenges: Children who have cognitive challenges may need extra time and multiple opportunities to explore how Loose Parts support their play, meaning making, and ideas. Children may engage more in object exploration before transitioning into more focused play. Remember that less is more; children will benefit from exploring more quantities of just one type of Loose Part at a time rather than a few of many different types of Loose Parts. Observe how children explore them. Do you notice a shift in the exploration? Does it seem that they are being more intentional in their exploration (such as positioning the Loose Parts to create art or stacking wooden blocks to build a tower)? Answers to these two questions may provide a cue as to when to introduce new Loose Parts into the ecosystem. For instance, Alfonzo, who has Down syndrome, enjoys the sound blocks make when you bang them together. He repeatedly places one block on top of another and knocks them down. His play and intention to stack keeps developing, and eventually he makes the important connection that he can stack two large hollow blocks against the fence and climb them. His interest in stacking helps him gain control of his need for climbing as he learns that he can use blocks to accomplish his goals.

Communication challenges: Children who experience communication challenges such as difficulties with speech and language may need support in learning to play with others. As you introduce the Loose Parts into the ecosystem, give each type a name and describe it. Sit next to the child who needs extra help communicating, and guide them in expressing their wants. Help other children learn simple sign language to support communication and collaboration. The more that children with communication difficulties play with other children, the more ways they will find to communicate their ideas and feelings.

Sensory perception: Sensory exploration helps children with diverse sensory perception and registration capacities process, obtain, analyze, and react to sensations. Children with sensory challenges such as visual or hearing limitations may need specific adaptations to find, identify, and access Loose Parts. Loose Parts enhance the process of exploring, discovering, and experimenting with their different senses. Natural Loose Parts promote the sense of smell, and when the Loose Parts are combined with water and sand, the combination enhances the sense of touch. Loose Parts for banging and shaking, such as gourds or metal cans, pots, and pans, promote hearing. Large Loose Parts such as planks, wooden crates, tires, and tree stumps support the vestibular (which helps us balance, by means of the inner ear) and proprioceptive (which helps us perceive and act upon the positioning of our bodies, stimulated through movement) senses. Jayme can slowly walk while holding on to an educator's hand. He sees other children climbing onto planks supported by tree stumps and points in excitement. The educator walks him over and holds his hand as he slowly climbs onto the planks. Ariana, an older girl in the program, comes over and holds Jayme's other hand to help him walk on the planks. Later the children give Jayme rope to hold on to as he climbs and walks on the planks.

Neurodiversity: Children with neurodiversity have ways of exploring and learning that are often seen as challenging behaviors. The children may be more playful and have a higher need and urge to move than children who are not neurodiverse. This is a positive quality; when children are given the opportunity to play without restrictions, they may become more creative, artistic, and skillful at tinkering. After all, play is one of the most important activities in which human beings engage. However, today's climate of accountability and standardized assessment has created perceptions that often confuse difference with deviance and behavior with identity. We tend to pathologize, exclude, and consequently label children. This is most prominent with children who do not conform to our expectations of behavior. Yet when children are engaged, interested, and motivated in play, their focus tends to improve, and behaviors perceived as challenging may change. When the focus shifts to appreciating their learning process and educators provide opportunities to engage in meaningful and active play, children thrive and acquire more self-regulatory behaviors. The question then becomes not "How do we fix children's behavior?" but "How do we engage children to feel competent and capable so that they see the power of social interactions?" We know behaviors are not resolved with rewards and punishments; instead, we must give children the opportunity to learn and adapt to different perspectives and social interactions. When we unconditionally accept children for their authentic selves, we can truly guide them to become powerful citizens of the world.

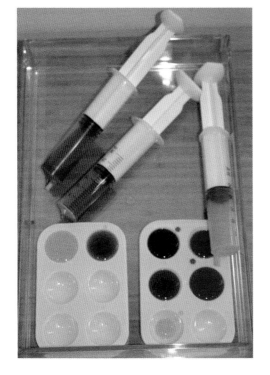

Hospitalizations: Children who are medically fragile may need extra care and consideration, but they benefit from the sense of normalcy play can bring to them. Just because they are in the hospital or staying home due to medical conditions does not mean their urge to play is gone. Educators and families must find ways to support their play and engage them in explorations that distract them from disruptive circumstances, discomfort, or fear. Many hospitals have family life specialists or child life specialists who serve as emotional support and help children and families develop coping strategies. With the support of educators and child life specialists, Loose Parts can create play opportunities and socialization activities that strengthen healthy interactions and friendly environments. Adaptable Loose Parts, art, and play help children express their anxieties about their diagnosis or procedures that they may not be able to otherwise verbalize and support them in making meaning about their experiences. Because Loose Parts are open-ended, they can enhance children's problem-solving and critical-thinking capacity, helping them understand what is happening and the procedures they may be going through. When my daughter Alexis was three years old, she was hospitalized for five days. The educators at Children Circle Nursery School came to visit her and brought items the children played with at the school. They also facilitated telephone conversations with other children and helped her process her hospital experience. At home we played with blocks; we built together and followed her lead as she engaged in dramatic play, using bandages to wrap her dolls and stuffed animals' knees. We added objects she could use to represent the procedures she endured. As a family, this powerful form of open-ended play relaxed us and deepened our understanding of the traumatic moment we all experienced. Alexis healed and continued to be the exuberant and playful child she was before her hospitalization.

The Educator's Role in Observing, Reflecting, and Supporting Play

The role of the educator is to be a researcher and learn along with the children and their families. We observe children to discover their interests and learn what inspires and motivates them. Take the time to engage in meaningful conversations and build trusting relationships. Observe them in natural environments without setting up activities that are meant to check off a specific assessment requirement. Reflect on how you can respond to children's interests and be open to learning along with them. Trust that co-constructing with children will increase your intentionality when you curate Loose Parts. Watch the story of growth that is unfolding and capture the powerful moments when new accomplishments are achieved. In Aotearoa New Zealand, early childhood programs use learning stories as a mode of formative assessment. Margaret Carr and Wendy Lee write in their book *Learning Stories in Practice*, "Stories of teaching and learning are at the heart of how we make meaning of our experiences" (2019, 2). When creating learning stories, educators conduct observation and assessment of children from a sociocultural perspective. Children are perceived as capable, competent, curious, engaging, innovative, caring, and empathic. In other words, their strengths and capacities are the focus of observation.

We all have memories of the stories we learned from our families. Stories are how we remember, think, communicate, understand, feel, and learn important values that guide our lives. American psychologist Jerome Bruner explains the importance of narrative in creating personal selfhood and identity in his book *Making Stories* (2003). Children with diverse abilities must have the same right as

all children to define their personhood and their identities through their stories of wonder, playful inquiry, and success, centering on their strengths and capacities. Opportunities for playfulness are enhanced within ecosystems that contain abundant invitations for story making and story sharing with Loose Parts and other thoughtfully curated materials. For example, peg people included in an outdoor storytelling playscape (a small dramatic play space) help Christopher tell the story of a weekend visit to see his cousins. A structure built using acrylic blocks becomes an airplane as Silvana describes her grandparents' upcoming visit. Acorns collected in the neighborhood become bunnies and kitty cats as Andrew and Niqui tell a story about taking care of animals.

Educators can take the time to recognize that there is a story behind every child and the story needs to lead our thinking and perceptions. Too often we create a narrative based on our own need to help or to hide our discomfort or lack of knowledge in supporting children with diverse abilities. Shifting away from these thought patterns requires critical reflection that starts with changing our existing narrative that children with diverse abilities have needs that must be solved by an adult. I propose a different narrative, one that disrupts our thinking and allows educators to live in disequilibrium and uncomfortableness, because it is the things that make us uncomfortable that give us the strength to disrupt the status quo and lead change. Ecosystems that transform the people who inhabit them are rooted in the ways we listen to one another and the profound consideration we show for all the strengths and capacities of the children, families, and communities that inhabit the ecosystem. When we are ready to see children as powerful learners and competent players regardless of their abilities, we can begin to create ecosystems where we can all grow and thrive to our utmost capacities. When we listen, learn, and co-construct knowledge along with the children, we grow as educators and humans. Sometimes it takes asking ourselves these questions:

- What images do I associate with the experience of children with diverse abilities?
- What images do I associate with children's ecosystems designed for equity, equality, and inclusion?
- How might these ecosystems support the lives of the world's most vulnerable children and those who support them?
- How would I create a transformative ecosystem that focuses on the strengths and capacities of children, families, and communities?

By observing children and reflecting on what we see with these perspectives in mind, we can begin to make thoughtful adaptations to the spaces and to the items with which they engage. Introducing Loose Parts into the environment can help us remain focused on what children are capable of instead of what they are not able to do. In other words, a child with diverse abilities may need extra support, but they also need the freedom to decide what to play and how to go about it. When they participate in Loose Parts play, they are using their full capacities to move, manipulate, and explore the materials. They are in charge of what they can do and how they can do it. The more opportunities we provide children with diverse abilities to engage in child-driven play, the more they can make key connections to their own initiative, emotions, and means of expression.

Designing Ecosystems That Create a Sense of Belonging

We need beauty in our lives and spaces in which we can share, create, and find inspiration. We need the harmony that the beauty of the human spirit can provide. We need spaces that are hopeful and say, "You belong," those that guide us to embrace our humanity and find strength in people. The English philosopher Roger Scruton (2009, 174) writes, "The experience of beauty guides us along this second path: it tells us that we are at home in the world, that the world is already ordered in our perceptions as a place fit for the lives of beings like us."

When we refocus our energy and intention to create spaces that embrace inclusion and equity, we create ecosystems, not just environments. We open the way for our collective imagination, our emotions become known, and respect and collaborative meaning making flourish. This is how we must approach inclusive spaces. An inclusive perspective recognizes that all children must be respected and supported, regardless of their abilities. They deserve and have the right to feel safe, actively participate in the community in which they live and learn, and feel a sense of belonging.

For children with diverse abilities to thrive, educators must be intentional in creating ecosystems that are accessible and inclusive, and that offer materials that engage children using multiple modalities. I am inspired by the definition of inclusion used in the schools of Reggio Emilia in Italy, where children with diverse abilities are considered children with special rights. The focus shifts from meeting the needs of children to recognizing that children have the right to receive support and needed accommodations so they can fully participate in the classroom and the family. In this shared ecosystem, a psychologist-pedagogista participates in adaptations and therapeutic services delivered in the classroom, and an extra educator supports the inclusion of the child with special rights as well as all the children in the classroom. Families are invited to participate in the whole ecosystem community. This inclusive approach has an emphasis on strengths and abilities, and it does not focus on any potential deficit from the disability. At the same time, children who are typically developing are better able to understand and accept differences (Hall et al. 2010).

Designing Ecosystems That Promote Empathy and Compassion

Empathy is the ability to recognize, appreciate, and respond to another person's feelings and perspectives. Empathy is a necessary part of learning to get along with others, and children have an amazing capacity for empathy. As typically developing children grow in cognitive ability, they begin to realize that other children need the support of a wheelchair, a hearing aid, or other tools to help them with day-to-day activities. They develop empathy, understanding, and compassion for children who need extra help.

An important consideration in promoting empathy involves our classroom rules and expectations. For instance, in many programs I have visited, there is a general rule that everyone is a friend and no one is allowed to turn away a child who wants to play. The intention is to reduce the hurt and harm of peer rejection. However, is the expectation that everyone is a friend realistic? Does this rule help children learn to express their interests, advocate for themselves, and build authentic relationships? In the following story, you can see how children are capable of forming friendships without being forced.

Genine is constructing a complex block structure (it appears to be a castle), verbalizing what she is doing. She wants to create a bridge that leads to the main building using Kodo geometric shapes and flat tree cookies. The uneven shapes present a challenge. Allan, who has some speech challenges, has been watching

Genine build the structure. He slowly says, "Put the tree cookie first." Genine hesitates and seems to be weighing whether she wants Allan to play with her. The educator comes close and says, "Allan, let Genine know you want to help her." Gradually, Allan asks Genine if he can play. Genine looks at him and says, "You can be a builder."

The educator helped Allan articulate his desire to play rather than forcing Genine to play with Allan. By focusing on helping Allan ask Genine if he could play, the educator was giving him tools that would support his ability to socialize.

Building empathy by helping children learn to play with one another is an important role of educators and families in equitable and inclusive environments. What a magnificent opportunity to create ecosystems where we can so profoundly listen to and learn from one another, finding connections between our stories and those of people who have lived experiences different from our own. There is power in challenging one another and imagining other perspectives—these opportunities touch our core. It is at the very heart of genuine curiosity that we develop empathy and compassion.

Educators can increase children's sensitivity toward their peers with diverse abilities by holding open discussions and by using Loose Parts in role play and dramatic play. In play settings, educators can encourage and point out instances

when children are being helpful or comforting to one another. By focusing on the children, rather than imposing rules, educators design authentic ecosystems that promote equity, equality, and inclusion.

Designing Ecosystems That Support Identity

To support the whole child, we must help them build their sense of self and identity. One way is by offering books in which they see themselves represented. A powerful practice is displaying photos of the children around the room to create documentation boards that support children's thinking and explorations. Take photos of children engaged in active exploration and mount them on small blocks so they can represent themselves in their play. Or add a magnet to the photos—children can move these across a magnet board as a visual representation of who is present that day. Mount photos on CD cases, and children can place them in a project they are working on so others know it's still in progress. The photographs not only serve to support children's identities but also help them organize their daily schedule and anticipate what is happening next. The mounted photographs become Loose Parts for play. They also invite children to engage in powerful conversations about differences and similarities.

In *Loose Parts 3: Inspiring Culturally Sustainable Environments,* we encourage educators to consider the impact of racism, ableism, ageism, heterosexism, and classism on children's lives. The book offers a variety of ideas for creating spaces that promote equity, even in homogeneous communities. In this book, I want to encourage educators and families to continue to reflect on their biases and take an active approach to prevent any bias from entering our work with children. We must consider intersectionality, a term coined by Kimberlé Crenshaw (1989) to describe the simultaneous experience of social categories such as race, gender, socioeconomic status, and sexual orientation and how these categories interact to create systems of oppression, domination, and discrimination. Now more than ever, we must create ecosystems that promote anti-racist and anti-ableist work.

Designing Ecosystems That Build Community

Nothing is more powerful than getting to know each family and child who enters your program. They bring traditions, histories, language, and cultures that enrich the tapestry of the ecosystem. Create opportunities that promote a sense of community where families can learn and can help and support one another. Hosting play days when families can relax and play together and with one another's children is a wonderful way to create community. I have beautiful memories of my own children's childhood when families gathered to build with blocks and play outdoors with sand, water, and natural Loose Parts. In the moments we spent together, we learned to appreciate the special capacities of every child, including the children with diverse abilities. All of us belonged, and every child was included. Invite families to share their traditions and how they celebrate milestones in their lives. This can be particularly important for families with children with diverse abilities who may be overwhelmed or experience moments of doubt for their children's future.

Micayla Whitmer, one of the advisory panel members who guided the writing of this book, shared this advice on becoming more aware about body language and being more inclusive. Children of all ages, regardless of their expressive language abilities, communicate their thoughts, feelings, and needs through their bodies. Educators can notice these movements (clenched teeth, hunched shoulders, frowns, open positioning of the shoulders and arms, smiles, a wide stance, and so on) and respond accordingly. By paying attention to what children's bodies are telling us, we can create an environment where children will thrive.

The role of educators and families is to create spaces where children with diverse abilities can explore freely along with other children. Children, adults, and families are interdependent, and when one person is triumphant, the rest of the community benefits. In inclusive ecosystems, all children, regardless of ability, race, language, culture, and ethnicity, deserve to actively contribute to the community and participate in democracy by being recognized for their capacities. Families and educators can achieve a vision of education based on strong values of equity and inclusion—where new ideas emerge to inspire new visions, values, and innovative practices. Many opportunities exist to support and encourage connections between children, educators, families, materials, the natural world, and ideas. Ecosystems must build upon these connections to strengthen creativity and innovation. Value the time you spend together and focus on relationships rather than curriculum and standards. Observe and listen and build upon children's knowledge. Offer children different ways to represent their thinking, such as stones to tell stories or a variety of art media to express their feelings. Educators and families can invite children to slow down, notice, and get lost in the flow of play. This is particularly important if children with diverse abilities experience frequent interventions that disrupt playfulness.

Designing Equitable, Equal, and Inclusive Ecosystems

Imagine an ecosystem designed to promote playfulness as an attitude of freedom, imagination, and joy (Armstrong 1998): ecosystems that are rich in possibilities for curiosity and discovery; ecosystems where children and adults get lost in play and wonderment; ecosystems where labels and disabilities do not exist and instead adults see children full of potential and with a deep desire to grow and be successful. Ecosystems that promote play need to be infused with Loose Parts that encourage children to wonder, explore, and create positive visions for an expectant future.

A foam handle on a rake makes it easier to grasp.

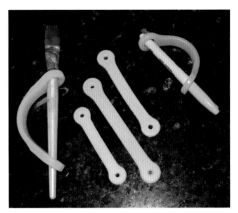
Adding silicone adaptive holders can facilitate tool use.

Inclusion must be a proactive and intentional process that helps set expectations and promotes success because it respects children's interests, ideas, and capacities while promoting agency (the power of self-motivation to reach a goal). Inclusion is grounded in a clear understanding of child development, including the development of children with diverse abilities, and in the principles of deep-rooted social justice, equity, and social inclusion. It recognizes that learning happens in the context of relationships, interactions, and experiences. An inclusive ecosystem intentionally creates opportunities for children with diverse abilities to engage in explorations that profoundly influence brain development and children's social-emotional well-being. Active exploration with Loose Parts helps remove labels by supporting and increasing the existing capacities of young children. The unpredictable nature of Loose Parts breaks down barriers and creates a more inclusive social process. For example, children with diverse abilities benefit when creating a collective fence weaving with other children, using rolls of Mylar paper. Children with diverse abilities may need some adult support with accommodations, provided with sensitivity so children have the maximum freedom to unleash their creativity. By making useful adaptations in an early childhood ecosystem, we create a place of belonging where equity, equality, and inclusion guide all our decisions and practices.

As adults who design ecosystems for children who show a variety of capacities and strengths, we must create opportunities for all children to engage in relationships and interactions that support their development and learning. Therapeutic interventions take place in the context of the naturalistic spaces where children belong, live, and play, and children with diverse abilities are acknowledged as playful scientists in search of wonder and inquiry. Ecosystems must offer children opportunities that range from engaging in concrete and hands-on explorations of Loose Parts to connecting abstract ideas among themes that emerge in their play. Imagine children with diverse abilities and picture their brains developing complex wiring as they engage in exploring clay, seed

pods, acorns, leaves, and flowers. Imagine children with diverse abilities actively exploring language when they engage in dramatic play. Think about the connections children make when they explore light and shadows using transparent and opaque Loose Parts.

Loose Parts help create ecosystems where children can connect their big ideas to their everyday interactions. To support children's innate drive to connect, see, and create relationships, adults can provide Loose Parts, art materials, and time to tinker. Adults can talk with children about what they see, celebrating novel ideas and taking delight in children's tremendous capacity to create and appreciating and encouraging the use of metaphor. Opportunities increase when educators and families value play and design with a playful attitude. I invite you to play, explore, and find the wonderment of Loose Parts. As you begin to design ecosystems of inclusion, start by observing children, reflecting on the following questions:

- What spaces within the ecosystem are most often visited and explored?
- What Loose Parts elicit the greatest delight?
- What accommodations would encourage freer exploration of Loose Parts?
- What spaces, experiences, or Loose Parts sustain children's interests and play for the longest periods of time?
- What questions do children seem to be asking as they discover new ways to use Loose Parts?
- What invitation can you add to the ecosystem to promote collaboration between children?

- Based on these observations, how can we create new inclusive and equitable opportunities for joy, wonder, and inspiration?
- Where do I, as an adult, find joy and freedom?

Creating opportunities where children with diverse abilities and children who are developing typically can play together promotes empathy and understanding. Educators and families can empower healthy relationships when they support and encourage children's social play and collaborative work. They help children understand feelings and make them visible by naming them and being curious about the behaviors associated with them. Educators and families can talk with children about the things they care about and let children see what it looks like to take action on behalf of those things. Educators and families can provide critical support for children to build awareness of unfairness in this world and help them learn to cope and respond appropriately.

Loose Parts build the brain's capacity to create, invent novel solutions, imagine and understand different perspectives, and communicate with care, courage, and compassion. We need these kinds of minds to create peaceful, inclusive, equitable, and sustainable ecosystems. Perhaps the best place to start inspiring these qualities in children is by asking the following questions:

- **About children:** Who are the children who inhabit the ecosystem? What are the ages and developmental stages of each child? What are they interested in? What capacities and contributions do they bring into the ecosystem?
- **To educators:** What do we want to know about each child and each family? How will we support the identity of every child? How will we create an ecosystem that values community? How do we communicate with one another? How do we create spaces for therapists, support staff, and families? What do we value about an ecosystem that promotes equity, equality, and inclusion? How do we define community? What are the children aware of in the world today? How are they talking and expressing their feelings about what they hear outside the classroom?
- **To families:** What do you want to know? How can we welcome you into the ecosystem? How do we authentically engage you in decision-making? How do we capture your family's capacities to enhance the learning ecosystem? How do we honor your language, history, traditions, and culture? What are your hopes?
- **To the community:** How do you define community? What events, invitations, and engaging explorations are available in the community (art events, theater, celebrations, and gatherings that focus on contemporary issues and challenges)? What resources are available for families who need support? How can we collaborate with resource agencies to ensure continuity of help?

How do we invite community members to engage and share knowledge and skills with children (elders, representatives of different cultures, artists, carpenters, musicians, and people who have a special right)?

As you answer these questions, you may see a framework emerging that will further support you as you design inclusive and equitable ecosystems. Embrace the process and allow yourself to develop a design lens that includes a strong vision:

- Children are capable, competent, curious, and the protagonists of their own knowledge.
- The ecosystem allows children with diverse abilities and all children to become contributing members.
- Explorations and the physical ecosystem design support relationships and create a sense of belonging and a sense of place.
- The ecosystem is deeply rooted in the values, mission, and vision of the program.

And finally, we ask ourselves, is this environment rich in possible relationships? Are there a variety of elements in the design, in terms of depth, dimension, and scale? Is it welcoming and safe? Is there variation in light and color, materials, and sensory information, including sounds and smells? Does it reflect a strong, rich, powerful image of children? How do these elements provide the possibility for creating a place where imagination thrives? Does it invite and create opportunities for exchanging ideas? For collaboration? Can any child discover more about themselves, their community, and the world, challenging and broadening their perspectives? Does it emphasize exploration, discovery, being comfortable with the unknown, and playing with possibilities, instead of seeking the "right" answer or certainty? In other words, does it communicate and invite exploring the complexity and richness of learning in the space between the known and unknown, between certainty and uncertainty?

The Study of Play in Children with Diverse Abilities

Educators and families can offer children with diverse abilities opportunities to use Loose Parts to explore art, play with numbers, tell stories, experience nature, test science, and learn about the world. It happens when we place play and joy at the center of all our practices, work, and desires. In play, the pleasurable emotions associated relax our brains and free them up for layered and multidimensional growth. When children with diverse abilities play, they have the best opportunity to make meaning and connections without the fear of making mistakes, not meeting adult expectations, or failing.

Before 1980 little research was conducted on the impact of play and the developmental process of play in young children with diverse abilities. Even when studies began to emerge, the methodology was flawed in that they focused on the disability and how it limited children, rather than focusing on play behaviors. Most of the studies also failed to control the play settings and the children's familiarity with play objects (Quinn and Rubin 2018). At almost the same time, the early childhood special education profession started to blend a more constructivist approach, which considers children as protagonists of their own learning, with developmental theory and behavioral learning. This new blend of perspectives led to more opportunities for research and practice. In the early 1990s, the focus on research shifted to stronger emphasis on play and a more holistic view of children with diverse abilities. Researchers such as Tony Linder (1993) introduced a more interdisciplinary approach to assessment and evaluation. Stanley Greenspan, Serena Wieder, and Robin Simons (1998) developed a framework that further emphasizes play as the focus of observation and assessment of children's strengths and abilities. Diane Bricker (Pretti-Frontezak and Brickner 2004), a professor of special education, author, and scholar, introduced the concept of activity-based early intervention, which proposes a strong focus on a child-initiated, naturalistic, and relationship-based approach to promote play in young children with diverse abilities. The activity-based intervention approach promotes the concept of inclusion by supporting the learning of children with diverse abilities in the social context of everyday activities—child care activities and routines, child-chosen and child-initiated play activities, and explorations intentionally designed and planned by adults to encourage play. Bricker applied the teachings of Lev Vygotsky, Jean Piaget, John Dewey, Dante Cicchetti, and Donald J. Cohen.

In the late 1990s, sociologist Judy Singer (2017), who is on the autism spectrum herself, coined the term *neurodiversity* to describe conditions such as ADHD, autism, and dyslexia. This shifted the focus from the deficit, disorder, and impairment to accepting diverse ways of processing, thinking, and learning. This approach proposes that differences are just differences and not deficits, opening the path for Universal Design for Learning (UDL). The goal of UDL is to infuse the ecosystem with opportunities, strategies, and methods to remove barriers that prevent growth, development, and learning. It shifts the focus toward children's strengths rather than meeting a need through remediation. Berry Mayall (2013), a specialist in childhood studies, suggests a shift from seeing developmental differences as problematic to increasing attention to children's agency, strengths, and identity.

In the twenty-first century, research on brain development opened further dialogue and new findings on the importance of play in childhood and beyond.

Researchers, including neuroscientist Jaak Panksepp (2014), present the idea that the function of play is to build the social brain. He argues that emotional processes, including experienced feelings, are key in the chain of events that control human actions.

Research on brain development informs the way we create inclusive ecosystems where children with diverse abilities can thrive. Through repetitive practice, the brain establishes connections that support children's understanding of the world. When repetitive practice is combined with emotions, feelings, and physical movements, children develop the skills that help them succeed. Ultimately, these skills take shape as ideas and interests that can be supported through provocations and inspirations using Loose Parts. As these ideas expand, the brain creates new pathways and innovative possibilities emerge. This is the principle of neuroplasticity, or the brain's ability to reorganize itself by forming new neural connections throughout life. With constant practice, children begin to establish a series of patterns and schemas that help them make sense of the world around them. These patterns become the root of each individual's overall growth and help move exploration and learning forward. Once children with diverse abilities have enough confidence in their basic abilities, they are more flexible and dynamic in their play. Examples of this process can be seen in block building, which starts with lining the blocks, stacking, and then bridging. In art, children progress through a sequence of mark making into more sophisticated drawings. Children become more flexible and more capable of adapting a familiar pattern to create new patterns and thus develop more neural pathways. It is this incredible capacity of the brain to re-create and reconnect neurons (nerve cells) that allows each child to make progress, compensate for challenges, and reach their full potential.

Neuroplasticity is related to the relevance, frequency, intensity, and sequence of experiences. It can be adaptive, as in the acquisition of a new skill, or maladaptive, as in the formation of a dependency or disorder. Research on neuroplasticity has supported the importance of early intervention, a child- and family-centered process that supports infants and toddlers with developmental delays by starting services early and increasing levels of support to ensure successful outcomes. Early intervention reinforces neuroplasticity by increasing the regeneration of neurons in the brain. Through play, social connections, and interactions with peers and adults, children with diverse abilities can create neuronal connections that help compensate for brain injury or other developmental delays. Loose Parts create complex and engaging ecosystems that support neuroplasticity by creating more neuronal connections. Physical activities such as dancing with scarves or ribbons also support the development of children's brains (Kolb, Harker, and Gibb 2017).

Moving beyond the Label

It is crucial to remind ourselves that as educators our role is not that of an expert on specific disabilities. Neither are we in the role of assessing and diagnosing. The purpose of this book is to support all children's capacities, interests, and ideas, regardless of their individual abilities. When children with diverse abilities engage in play, they can grow and move beyond the label they have been assigned by an assessment specialist. Labels group children into standardized disability boxes without considering their unique capacities, interests, and abilities. Labels shift the focus toward observing and assessing symptoms and deficits, rather than promoting children's existing strengths. With that in mind, this book is not written to suggest adaptations for specific disabilities. Instead, we propose that children with diverse abilities, regardless of any diagnosis, benefit from sustainable play using Loose Parts. Adaptations are suggested to increase accessibility and to promote a more inclusive approach to using the Loose Parts educational philosophy to engage children with diverse abilities in sustainable play.

The focus of this book is to support educators and families to see beyond the limitations and instead notice the strengths of children with diverse abilities. Remember to focus on what children can do rather than what they can't. It is crucial to avoid losing play's value in favor of accessibility; simply being able to do something isn't what makes exploration enjoyable. Play needs to be freely chosen, child-directed, and intrinsically motivated. In other words, a child with diverse abilities might need a little support, but they also need the freedom to decide what they want to play with and how they want to play.

As children engage with Loose Parts, we notice the joy and exhilaration they feel in the flow of play. When we challenge children to take initiative, they develop a deeper understanding of who they are, what they want, and what they are capable of. When we remove labels and centralize play in promoting development, we can spark children's curiosity and their hope for a more prosperous future that is not determined by the characteristics of a diagnosis. Thus, play equity is achieved.

We must acknowledge that children need to be children first, not identified by their disability or condition. Families and educators can provide plentiful and intriguing explorations that stimulate, challenge, and support children with diverse abilities to grow and develop. Ecosystems, whether at home, in the classroom, or in the hospital, must practice freedom and hope regardless of their location. If we strive to have a society that is grounded in respect, collaboration, and interdependent interactions, children must be fully visible and their voices must be heard. We must reflect on our ecosystems and avoid creating places that exclude children from play. All children need to be part of a community where they belong, where they can be free to be their authentic selves. We need a paradigm shift so that children who are being labeled with a disorder are instead recognized for the amazing people they truly are. We should take their cue and learn to be more playful in our own lives, regardless of our age. We must regard them not as individuals who need fixing but as wonderfully diverse children who can move us away from our dogmatic thinking. We must acknowledge their capacity to transform society.

How This Book Is Organized

This book is organized into chapters containing beautiful photographs of Loose Parts provocations, inspirations, and invitations designed to engage children in play. Throughout each chapter, I include anecdotes about children with diverse abilities that are grounded in the traditions of storytelling. The stories shared in the book are real stories either shared by families or observed by educators or myself during the years I have worked supporting children with diverse abilities. The stories highlight children's strengths, capacities, and learning and portray a powerful narrative of curiosity, inquiry, and their abundant capacities for learning. The stories are made for sharing and thus further promote equity and inclusion. They capture the magic of interactions to connect and engage families, educators, and children. Stories are particularly important for children with diverse abilities because they support identity formation, the connection of cognition, and sociocultural development. Because of the COVID-19 pandemic, it was not possible to photograph children in early childhood education (ECE) environments. Instead, I collaborated with ECE programs to visit them during the weekend or late afternoons when children were not present. Considering that families will also benefit from this book, photography also took place in a variety of home environments. I am thankful for the support of Casey Johnson and Debbie McMannis, educators at Lincoln Community Preschool, who agreed to photograph the children as they played with the Loose Parts brought over on the weekend.

Our work as educators is enhanced by collaboration. We are not individually the holders of all knowledge. Being able to consult, learn, and explore in collaboration creates collective intelligence. For this book, I gathered a group of colleagues to advise me, provide critical reflection, and challenge me to consider how best to support children with diverse abilities. I have reached out to mentors, colleagues, and friends who have expertise in supporting children. Their guidance is incorporated throughout the book, and I am positive it will inspire you as you consider designing inclusive and equitable ecosystems infused with Loose Parts. Rachel Marks, an occupational therapist, was instrumental in helping me with the accommodations and skills shared in this book. I highly recommend that you gather a group of critical friends with diverse expertise. Create an advisory council that can offer you specific ideas for accommodations and best ways to design ecosystems of equity and inclusion.

In consultation with this advisory group, I have carefully curated the Loose Parts shown in this book to support children who are typically developing as well as children with diverse abilities. Each photo setup contains a box with explanations about the materials, and many suggest accommodations. Because the purpose of this book is to portray inclusive ecosystems that focus on the strengths of children, the book is not organized by specific disabilities but instead structured to facilitate the creation of these ecosystems.

In this book, I also include key reflective questions to promote intentionality. As educators, how can we design an ecosystem where children and adults come together and create spaces where everyone feels welcome and invited to contribute to the community? How can we, together, create a place that invites us to be our authentic selves, an ecosystem where we want to play, learn, and contribute? I encourage you to start designing and selecting Loose Parts by asking reflective questions that can deepen your intention.

Chapter 2
Engaging the Senses

Sight, touch, hearing, and smell are integral parts of our memories. Our senses create feelings of belonging and comfort. When we cook and bake foods from our childhood, we are not only engaging the sense of smell but also bringing up a memory. When we look at the colors of a work of art, we are not only using our sight and vision but also awakening our emotions and perceptions surrounding the art, which may inspire or repulse us. When we touch fabric at a store, we are testing how it will feel next to our bodies—will it be scratchy or soft? When we hear a musical symphony or the rain hitting our window, we react differently based on our experiences. Also consider the proprioceptive system, located in our muscles and joints, which helps develop body awareness and serves as a regulatory system that assists in controlling responses to stimuli. The proprioceptive system can help in calming a child who is overwhelmed with stimulation. It can also alert a child who needs increased sensory stimulation to focus their attention on their play or exploration.

While stimulating the senses can be enjoyable, it also strengthens connections in the brain that enhance learning. Carefully curated Loose Parts engage children with diverse abilities in using their senses, stimulating sensory perception and enabling them to develop their powers of sensory discrimination. We use discriminatory skills for identifying similarities and differences as well as categorizing objects.

It is crucial to remember that children, regardless of ability, experience sensory exploration in their own way. Children may seek a variety of sensory explorations, or they may refuse all contact with certain materials. Sensory reactivity can cause a child to misinterpret emotional information from others, resulting in inappropriate and sometimes extreme emotional reactions (Greenspan, Wieder, and Simons 1998). Children who are overly sensitive to sensory input may need less stimulation and extended time to feel and sense experiences. It may take time for them to perceive differences and for the brain to effectively translate sensory stimulation into information. Reducing the intensity of background stimuli supports children with diverse abilities' growth and development because the sensory input affects their physical, socioemotional, and cognitive abilities. In many instances, extraneous stimuli need to be toned down so that children with diverse abilities can perceive specific stimuli and the brain can process the information.

When we observe children and carefully introduce Loose Parts into the ecosystem, they provide sensory benefits, including the following:

Cognitive development: Children compare characteristics of different Loose Parts. They develop an understanding of how things move and how they can use their bodies to move items. Discovering how a Loose Part feels, smells, and sounds helps children identify ways to use it. Cedar rings and cedar blocks stimulate the sense of smell. Transferring jingle bells from one container to another provides auditory stimulation.

Social skills: Children watch how others play, copy, and share ideas. Spaces where children build together using different types of blocks (natural blocks, unit blocks, KAPLA blocks, Dr. Drew's Blocks, tree cookies, and miniature tree stumps) provoke the senses and foster collaborative play and friendships.

Self-awareness: Children learn which Loose Parts they like and dislike. They test their hypotheses, interpret results, and make changes. These skills help them understand themselves and their capacities.

Physical development: Sensory activities develop the smaller muscles in hands and fingers (fine-motor control) and the larger muscles in legs, arms, and torso (gross-motor skills).

Emotional development: Sensory play is a relaxing and healthy way to release energy. It can help children with diverse abilities get in a state of flow, fully immersed in a feeling of energized focus, full involvement, and enjoyment in the process of play.

Communication skills: Whatever their level of language development, children can express how they feel about the Loose Parts with which they are playing. They may smile as they hold a soft scarf or laugh as they transfer water from one container to another. Children also offer ideas to one another, such as when designing a castle or building a bridge with blocks.

Look around the environment and notice the source of every stimulus. Consider the colors, the decorations on the walls, the flooring, the pillows, and the items on the shelves. Quietly sit in the empty space, close your eyes, and listen to the sounds. Take a deep breath and notice the smells. Walk around and take note of the colors, the number of materials available, the containers used, and items' accessibility. Take photos for reference and write notes about how you feel in the space. Notice what you touch and how you feel as you touch it. Perhaps, after an hour, start reading a book and concentrate on understanding its content. Are you unable to process the information efficiently? Does it take time to organize your thoughts? Do you continue to notice the stimuli around you? If you answer yes to any of the questions, take a second look at how the environment is designed and work on reducing stimuli. If it is overwhelming to you, imagine how it affects children who have immature regulation skills and children with diverse abilities.

In the past, the prevailing belief in early childhood education was that children needed colorful spaces to learn. Psychology researchers Anna Fisher, Karrie Godwin, and Howard Seltman (2014) of Carnegie Mellon University looked at kindergarten classroom displays to determine whether they affected children's ability to focus during instruction and learn the lesson content. They found that 85 percent of children in highly decorated classrooms were more distracted, spent more time off task, and demonstrated smaller learning gains than when the decorations were removed.

Now that you have taken the time to feel, experience, and explore your early childhood space, create a list of items to modify to create a space with fewer unnecessary stimuli. Your efforts to accommodate children's sensory needs and help them master challenges will make a difference in their ability to enjoy your company and learn. Remember that all children benefit from an environment that is designed with careful consideration for sensory integration. Simple modifications can substantially increase children's engagement and participation.

Key Reflections

- What do you notice about how each child in your ecosystem uses their senses?
- What provocations, invitations, or inspirations will you offer children to increase the use of their senses?
- What challenges do you notice that need to be considered as you integrate Loose Parts into the ecosystem to support the use of the senses?
- What types of Loose Parts can you infuse into the ecosystem to support the physical development of children with diverse abilities?

"I Want Fishy"

As an infant, Niqui learned to use baby sign language to express her needs and found creative ways to combine signs. When she wanted Goldfish crackers, her favorite snack, she put her index finger and thumb together to signify *small* and then make her mouth simulate how fish move their mouths when they eat.

When she started attending an early childhood program, she wore hearing aids. Before Niqui began school, the educators ensured that the children knew what sign language is and how it is used to communicate. They let the children try different hearing aids. They brought a wooden movable hand with books on sign language for the children to practice simple signs. The educators taught the children sign language to go with a made-up song about Goldfish crackers. They invited Niqui to visit the classroom and sing and sign the piece. After a few visits, Niqui felt welcomed and trusted the educators enough to stay without her parents. Niqui became a vital member of the community, teaching children new signs to communicate with her.

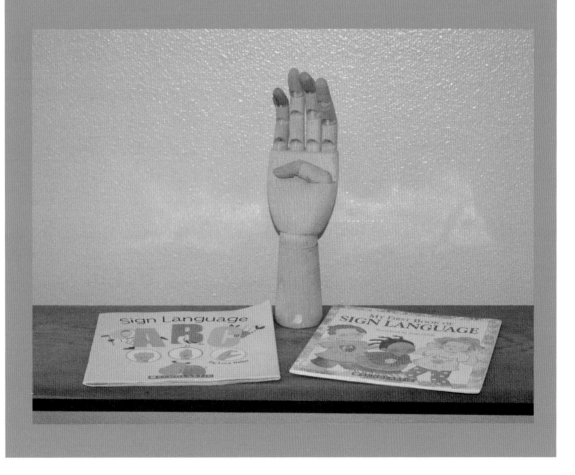

Try offering wider tongs, such as mini metal strawberry tongs or easy-to-squeeze plastic tongs, which may be easier to pick up materials with. Even using fingers to transport items greatly benefits fine-motor skills. When mini ziplock bags are difficult to open, use small tins or other containers instead.

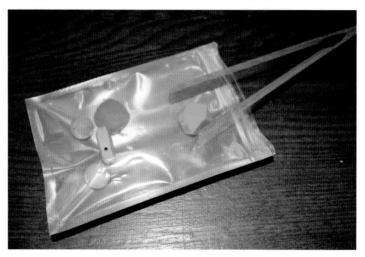

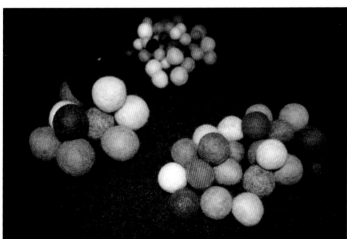

These multi-sized felted balls promote sensory exploration as well as visual discrimination. They are aesthetically inviting and offer a soft, rich feel for children who seek tactile input or are developing greater tolerance for different textures.

Scooping mini lights into clear boxes promotes visual attention and visual motor skills and is an exciting way for children to explore light and dark. For children who seek additional visual input to self-regulate, light and color exploration can offer a needed brain break.

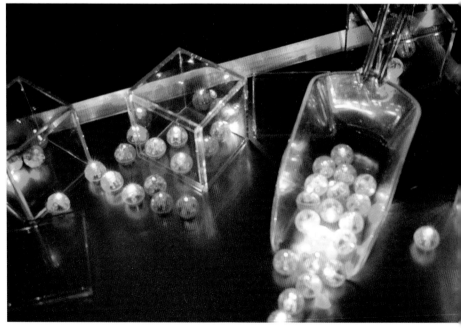

Sight and Vision

Watching a beautiful sunrise or a magnificent sunset as colors slowly change from bright oranges to dimmed soft peaches is fascinating. We notice the flowers as we take a walk, and we wonder at the breathtaking array of colors. We marvel at the transparency and opacity of a stained-glass window. Playing with light, color, transparency, opacity, contrast, and backgrounds can alter our perceptions and understanding of who we are and how we notice the world around us. But imagine children with diverse abilities who are unable to see or perceive details and differences in backgrounds and textures or who are not able to appreciate and recognize colors. So we must ask: How do we create ecosystems where all children participate in seeing, perceiving, and connecting? What can we do to include children who are blind or experiencing other vision and sight challenges? What invitations and provocations can we present to children with diverse abilities to explore sight and vision?

Before we discuss how to infuse Loose Parts to engage sight and vision, it is crucial to gain a deeper understanding of sight and vision and how they affect development and learning.

- Sight is the product of many components of the complex visual system. Sight is the physical and sensory experience that occurs when light reflects off an object. The light signals are perceived by the eyes and then sent to the brain to be converted into images.
- Vision is a learned process that evolves over time. It starts at birth and develops based on experiences and reactions to the environment. Vision is a thought process that emerges as an understanding of what is seen, where the object is, and how to react to it. Vision combines information from multiple sensory systems to create our perception of reality.

Sight allows a person to witness an event, but vision helps the person understand the significance of that event and draw interpretations. Sight and vision are harmonious and bring beauty and understanding of the world to us. They also keep us safe by allowing us to judge the potential risk in a situation. Allow me to share a personal story. I have vision challenges that affect my depth perception, which caused me to break my nose a couple of times playing volleyball in high school. I struggled with perceiving when the ball could hit me, so I usually did not have my hands ready to block the ball and it hit me straight in the face. However, my sight was sharp until I reached middle age. I still lack depth perception, but I have learned to accommodate by using various techniques (including not playing volleyball!).

Sight and vision keep our minds sharp and alert. Frequent stimulation of the mind and practice interpreting one's sense of vision improve overall health and intelligence. Now let's consider children who experience challenges with sight or vision. How does the environment affect their interactions with other children and adults and their connections to the world around them? Remember that the visual process's ultimate purpose is to arrive at an appropriate motor or cognitive response.

As educators, it is helpful to understand the skills children develop when they use both sight and vision. Since these components are crucial to children's development and learning, I outline them here in more detail.

Visual perception refers to the brain's ability to make sense or give meaning to what we see. Visual perception skills are essential for navigating our world and making sense of objects, letters, shapes, and numbers. Visual perception also affects motor coordination and motor abilities. Five-year-old David struggles with visual perception. He walks around the living room, sees an object on the floor, stops in front of it, and still trips and falls. He can see the object, but his brain struggles to perceive the object and send a message to the rest of his body to walk around or jump over it.

How the eyes move and collect information is known as visual processing. This facilitates how we take in information, how we make sense of it, and how it supports meaning making. It includes eye-hand coordination, tracking, convergence (eyes working together), visual fixation, and visual attention. Part of visual processing is concerned with optical efficiency (the effective use of visual information).

Loose Parts support visual-motor integration as children practice coordinating their body movements with what their eyes perceive. For example, Rogelio and his sight therapist play with inserting textured papers into tissue boxes. This helps Rogelio exercise his sight and vision. He carefully picks up a strip of paper with his right hand and brings it close to his eyes. Rogelio touches the tissue box with his left hand as he moves his right hand to the box and drops the paper into the opening. He turns around, smiles, and claps. Rogelio has learned to use both hands to guide him as he inserts Loose Parts into containers. This simple play sequence with Loose Parts supports his interest in inserting and strengthens his sight and vision.

Visual memory is the ability to store visual information in short-term memory and is a precursor to reading and writing. Classifying and sorting Loose Parts supports the development of visual memory, as children visually store images of items they are looking for when scanning to locate specific Loose Parts or images. Setting provocations that combine a Loose Part such as shells with a book or photograph of shells can support children with diverse abilities in making connections and storing visual memories for the future (long-term memory).

Visual closure is the brain's ability to recognize a familiar object even when only one part is displayed. Visual closure helps children quickly identify words by sight, which is key in learning to read. Visual closure helps children recognize inferences and predict outcomes. Small tray sandboxes with different textures of Jurassic Sands or similar play sand and various sticks, brushes, and craft sticks engage children in drawing and completing what they see. Provide images that show half of an object to invite children to predict what the other side is. Flat wood shapes invite children to match them or to create other shapes. For example, a triangle connected to another triangle makes a square or a rectangle. But remember to respect children's interest in play rather than our interest in teaching concepts.

Form constancy is the ability to recognize objects regardless of their orientation. Placing ordinary objects in positions that are different from the norm also helps children develop form constancy. Cut cardboard carpet tubes lengthwise to make two half tubes that look like a C and cover with Mylar on the inside or the outside to make a half reflective circle. Then invite children to explore reflection and distorted images as they place Loose Parts in front of the tubes. Children can also use Loose Parts to create self-portraits as they explore their faces in mirrors.

Perceiving visual-spatial relationships allows us to recognize and understand the relationships between objects within the environment and how they relate to us. Spatial awareness helps us know the distance between objects so we can avoid collisions. This skill helps children reach out and pick up an item, fill a container with Loose Parts, and calculate how far to jump. For instance, Shonte pulls three different sizes of cups from the shelf. She uses a measuring spoon and begins to transfer buttons from the basket to each of the cups. She counts how many scoops she pours into the cup, "One, two, three. I think I need three scoops in every cup." She continues to fill the next cup and counts, "One, two, three, four. Oops, I need four." She dumps the buttons into the basket and starts again. Shonte has not considered the buttons' or cups' varying sizes because her spatial awareness is still developing. Exploring the size, shape, and qualities of objects in relation to one another and herself will continue to improve Shonte's visual-spatial acuity.

The ability to distinguish details in an image or determine differences between two objects or two visual representations is visual discrimination. This practical skill arises in daily activities, recognizing shapes, numbers, and letters. It also includes visually noticing the properties of an object, such as smoothness, hardness, or roughness.

Figure-ground perception is the ability to distinguish objects from the background. Deficits in this area affect children's ability to understand images because important information gets lost when children cannot focus and find objects on specific background surfaces. Creating explorations with contrast and using materials with less visually busy backgrounds can increase children's ability to differentiate an item from a background.

Children who have visual challenges may need adults to guide them through tactile modeling, a technique in which the adult or peer guides the child to touch and manipulate objects to demonstrate how they can be used. They may also enjoy exploring different textured papers, such as bumpy, corrugated, and rough. Blocks can be organized by placing a sandpaper shape on a shelf, which assists children who are partially sighted in learning where to put the blocks away.

Children develop visual-motor integration and fine-motor manipulative skills by hooking and looping small metal clips. Hanging the tray in a vertical position rather than setting it on a table can assist children in grasping and precisely manipulating the hooks to fit into the holes.

The black and white canvases and acrylic pieces call attention to contrast, making this an appropriate exploration for children who see only certain colors or have decreased vision. It also supports visual spatial skills as children fill the containers and form creative visual designs.

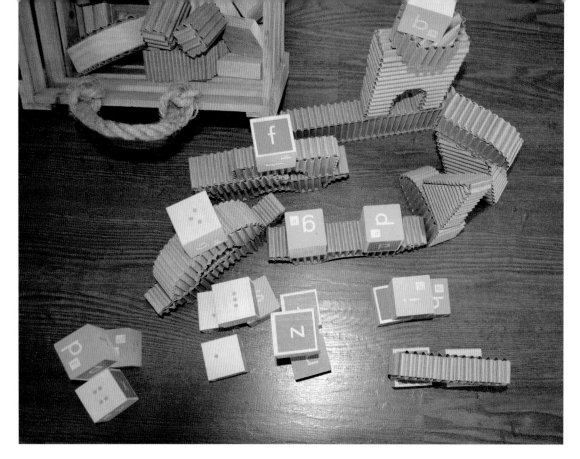

Corrugation adds texture for increased sensory input. These cardboard blocks, in combination with braille blocks, are an appropriate exploration for both typically developing children and children with diverse sight and vision abilities.

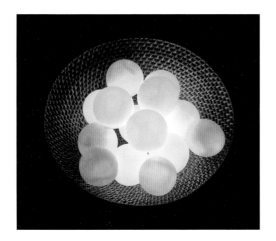

The soft glow of these color-changing light balls encourages exploration of color and light. Similar single-color lights may be appropriate for children who have a lower threshold for visual input from blinking or other brightly lit items.

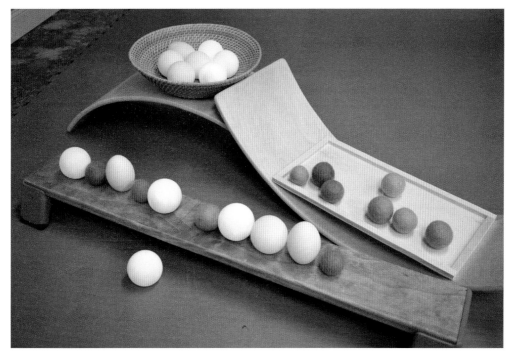

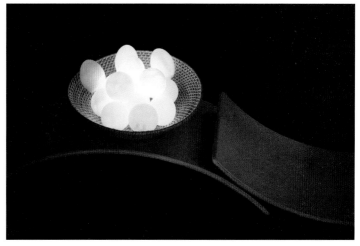

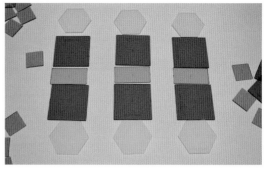

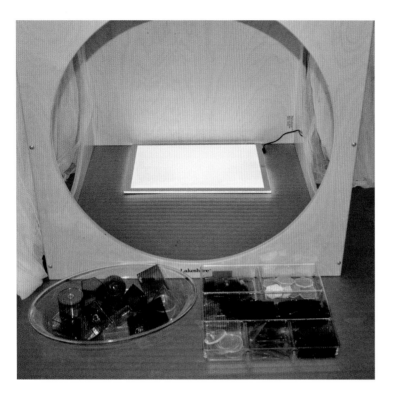

For children who can see shadows or those who see best under brighter light, you may accommodate by setting colorful 3D acrylic shapes on a regular tabletop or a tray with a solid contrasting color. Use a light table or a localized light such as a flashlight to highlight an object.

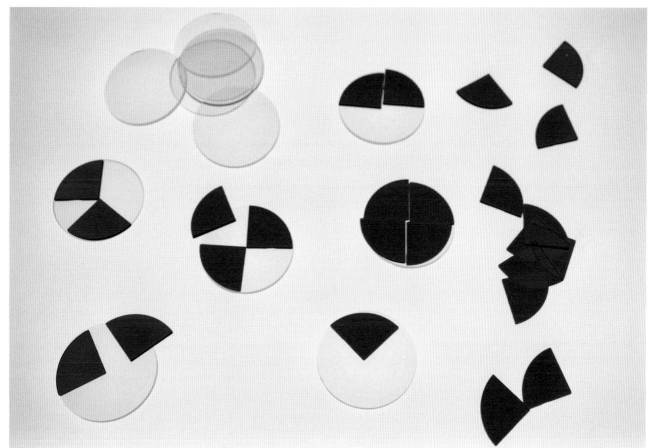

Hearing

Imagine the typical sounds of daily life. You hear birds chirping, the sound of the wind, or the subtle, muffled noise of traffic in the city. At night you hear the creaks of the house as it settles or the sound of crickets. These sounds give us comfort and embrace us in a sense of security. We know our space and we have a solid sense of place. For example, as we lived through this pandemic, we banged on pots, pans, spoons, and other Loose Parts, hoping that the grateful sounds we made at exactly the same time each day would relate our appreciation for the health care workers. That is the power of hearing, listening, and connecting. Deaf children and children who are hard of hearing do not experience music or nature sounds in the same way as someone without hearing impairments. However, there are many ways to include all children in the daily life of an early childhood education ecosystem. We can begin to design ecosystems that are equitable and inclusive by asking the following:

- How do we create ecosystems where children with diverse abilities participate in listening, hearing, and connecting?
- What can we do to include deaf children and children who are hard of hearing?
- What Loose Parts invitations and provocations can we present to children with diverse abilities to explore the sense of hearing?

Let's begin by understanding how we hear. The process of hearing requires changing sound waves into electrical signals that can be deciphered by the brain. Hearing loss is a general term referring to reduced functioning of the ear that affects the intensity and clarity of the sound we hear. The outer ear picks up a sound, and it travels through the ear canal into the eardrum. The eardrum vibrates, sending the sound to the three tiny bones (the malleus, incus, and stapes) in the middle ear. They amplify the vibrations and send them to the cochlea, a fluid-filled part of the inner ear. An elastic partition splits the inner ear into an upper and lower part and serves as the base for the hearing structure. The vibration reaches the fluid inside the cochlea, causing it to ripple, which creates a sound wave that travels through the inner ear. Sensory hair cells sitting near the wide end of the cochlea detect sharp sounds, while lower-pitched sounds are detected by the cells closer to the center. As the hair cells move up and down, stereocilia (hairlike projections) bump against the ear structure and bend. Bending causes the pore-like channels at the tip of the stereocilia to open. Chemicals rush into the cells, creating an electrical signal. The auditory nerve carries this electrical signal to the brain and turns it into a sound we recognize and understand (U.S. Department of Health and Human Services 2018).

With the understanding that sounds are made of different frequencies (pitch) and intensities (loudness), educators and families can intentionally create spaces where children interact without interruptions. Observe and notice children's reactions to sounds. How do they react to your voice, nature sounds, music, or many people speaking at once? Test different levels, from lower to higher pitch and softer to louder sounds. Through observation and consultation, you can notice if there are hearing challenges and how loud a sound must be for a child to hear. Are there sensorineural hearing challenges, the type of hearing loss that causes speech to be softer and less distinct?

Seek knowledge from the Deaf community to learn about Deaf culture, hearing loss, and deafness. This will support you in creating an inclusive and equitable environment. There is no better way to build such an ecosystem than through designing Loose Parts play opportunities. Play, especially symbolic play, is a powerful tool for improving language, cognition, self-regulation, and social interactions. These abilities can be specifically helpful for children like Joseph, a four-year-old who has no hearing in his right ear. He uses few words and wears a hearing aid. He spends a lot of time in the dramatic play area, exploring different roles and imagining complex play sequences. He is very skilled in symbolic representation and uses jacaranda pods, acorns, and small pine cones to make food, which he offers to other children nearby. Joseph is very social, and the educators use many strategies to engage all the children in visually representing their ideas. The children know that when they talk to Joseph they have to position themselves closer to his left ear so he can hear them.

Sophia, who is five years old and has limited hearing, enjoys spending time designing with a variety of Loose Parts. Raylin joins her at the table as they both design with glass beads. Sophia notices how Raylin uses the beads to create a mandala. Sophia starts creating a mandala using different colors. Both girls spend time watching each other's mandalas grow. They offer different colors of beads to each other. Raylin knows that Sophia has a hard time hearing, so she uses a louder voice and limits the words she uses. Sophia smiles as she carefully turns her head to hear what Raylin is saying. Using Loose Parts to create art provides Sophia another language to express her thinking and ideas. She is skilled at transferring her transient art into representations using paper and paint. Her sophisticated drawings serve as another form of communication.

When gathering to sing, play musical instruments, or make beautiful noise, include Loose Parts that children can feel vibrating so that they can participate and follow the rhythm. Dr. Dean Shibata, assistant professor of radiology at the University of Washington School of Medicine, discovered that deaf children sense vibrations in their auditory cortex and that sounds and musical vibrations are processed in the same part of the brain in deaf and hearing people. This may be the reason that musicians can sense the rhythm and vibrations as they write

music and deaf people enjoy attending a concert. It is the nature of the information, not the mode by which it is received, that seems to be important to the developing brain (University of Washington 2001). Take Ariana, who is deaf, and is often seen dancing with scarves and drumming in the sound garden. She aligns cans according to size. She holds each can with her open hand and uses her other hand to bang it with a metal spoon. She carefully feels the vibration and laughs. Educators take tempered glass containers and fill them with water. They invite the children to watch as they gently tap the containers with a wooden spoon. The children notice the ripples and vibrations and want to test different ways they can make the water vibrate. Ariana is particularly interested in this exploration and asks questions and shares her ideas using sign language. In this exploration, all the children contribute and help Ariana feel accepted and included.

We must also consider children's reactions to loud and soft sounds. Some children have functional hearing but fail to respond to sounds around them due to hypersensitivity, decreased auditory awareness, or intense focus on a task. Some children are sensitive to loud noise to the extent that they become dysregulated and seek refuge under a table or behind a chair. Contrarily, some children need sound and constantly seek auditory stimulation. They hum during a sing-along or independent work on an art project, talk loudly and exuberantly, and go around the classroom drumming on objects.

Language is everywhere in our classrooms, and there are ways to make it accessible for all children. According to advisory member Micayla Whitmer, American Sign Language (ASL) is the primary language of the American Deaf community. There is a difference between cultural Deafness and the medical view of deafness, and as such the specific needs of Deaf/deaf children vary depending on what language modality they use (ASL, spoken English, or both). If you have a child in your classroom whose primary language modality is sign language (and they do not have an interpreter), there are ways to involve the whole classroom in inclusive language. Introducing signs to children can facilitate both teacher-to-child communication and child-to-child communication. It is important to note the difference among "baby signs," stand-alone signs, ASL, and other types of sign language like Pidgin Signed English or Black American Sign Language. Although what you are providing is not a language (and accommodations for language use should be discussed with parents), it can be used as a communication system for the whole classroom.

Remember that sound is produced through vibrations. While some children process these vibrations auditorily, other students process vibrations corporally. Creating spaces for children to interact with vibrations through their bodies opens new avenues for learning. Changing the frequency or amplitude of sound vibrations provides a sensory experience for all children. Noise-canceling headphones can encourage children who are in the process of adapting to new sensory experiences to explore and feel safe around the sounds. Have headphones available throughout the ecosystem for all children to use to manage auditory input.

Children may select provocations with pronounced sounds, such as jingle bells, to increase their alertness and self-regulation.

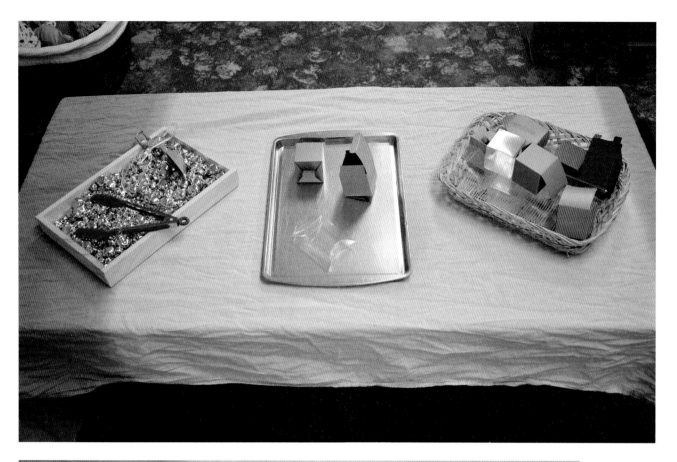

Filling jars and tubes with colorful abalone pieces, sand, and rocks creates an abundance of sounds. Try incorporating fillings of different textures and combining the containers with other Loose Parts to motivate children in developing bilateral coordination (using two sides of the body together in an activity) and visual-motor integration skills.

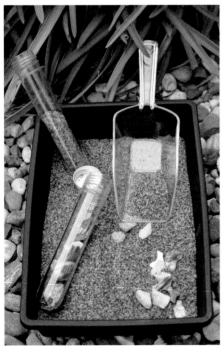

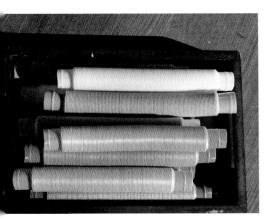

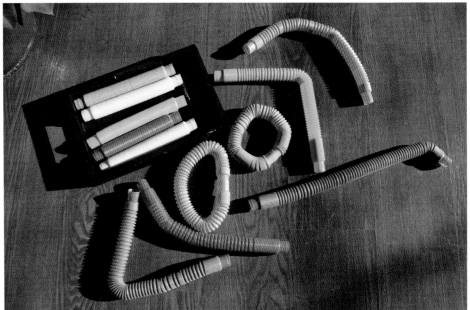

These corrugated tubes make a delightful popping sound when pulled apart and pushed together. Because they are lightweight and cylindrical, children with low muscle tone can grasp and manipulate them. For children who have more function in one hand, stabilize the tube on a surface so they can make fun sounds and shapes using one hand.

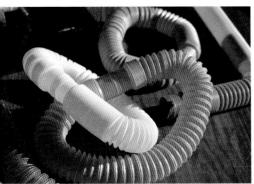

Pots, pans, spoons, balls, and corrugated metal items work well for rubbing or banging to create sounds and vibrations. Children can feel the vibration through a whisk as it strikes the metal materials.

All children, including deaf children and children who are hard of hearing, can test out varying sounds or vibrations on each nested wooden box using wooden tongs, spoons, and other utensils.

Touch

We live in a world of rich tactile experiences: raindrops falling on our skin, the hardness of a piece of wood, the gentle caress of a loved one, and the softness of a silky fabric. We know that touch is a basic human need. It is that natural instinct that provides emotional security and human connection. The sense of touch refers to every physical sensation that can be felt through the skin, which has separate nerves to register coldness, heat, pain, and pressure. With our sense of touch, we can tell objects apart and interpret the variety of stimuli that comprise the richness of the world. Our sense of touch is a high-functioning machine that decodes stimuli and gives us a remarkable capacity to recognize objects, discriminate textures, and engage in social relationships.

Touch affirms the concept of loving and being loved. Infants thrive when they are lovingly touched and held by family members. When touch is given thoughtfully and unconditionally, families, educators, and children form bonds that last a lifetime. But what happens when children do not want to be touched and prefer not to engage in tactile stimulation? Then there are children who need to touch everyone and everything, seeking out tactile sensory input. Let's spend time unpacking the sensory system and reasons why some children are resistant to certain types of touch.

The largest organ in our bodies is the skin, and it is composed of mechanoreceptors, a sense organ or cell that responds to mechanical stimuli such as touch or sound vibrations (Iheanacho and Vellipuram 2019). Pain and touch are intricately related, and insights into pain processing can help us understand the fundamental principles of typical touch. A recent study by researchers from Johns Hopkins University School of Medicine divides nonpainful touch into two basic categories. Each type of touch is detected by different neurons in the skin and ultimately activates different regions of the brain (Abraira and Ginty 2013):

- **Discriminative:** This allows us to touch an item and sense its pressure, shape, texture, and vibration. For example, a child reaching inside a bag of Loose Parts can discern what they are by touching them.
- **Affective:** This is closely linked to social or emotional touch. It senses slow stroking and temperature. Affective touch is what makes a caring touch from an adult or another child feel pleasant.

To respect children's sensitivity to touch, start by introducing Loose Parts that are familiar, and observe their reactions. As you notice a child is more receptive, introduce new Loose Parts slowly. Notice if they prefer the texture, weight, or shape of different Loose Parts. The most important thing is to know the children and recognize if there are times when touch feels painful. For instance, Alina is three years old and sensitive to rough surfaces. She won't wear pants with zippers or any item of clothing that has labels or sewn edges. She prefers soft cotton and refuses to wear any items that are too heavy. She often tugs on her clothes as if they are causing pain and reacts strongly to smells, which increase her discomfort, making her cry and sit in a corner rocking. She enjoys sitting on the floor with a basket of small wooden blocks that she stacks and lines up in different configurations. The educators noticed that Alina accepted the hard surface of the blocks, so they gradually incorporated sanded-smooth tree cookies, small tree stumps, and wooden spools. They made sure that there were no specific smells. As Alina became more comfortable in her play, they considered what softer items they might introduce and settled on soft yarn felted balls that they could wash to take smells away. It took some time for Alina to touch them, but eventually she began sorting them inside colorful wooden rings. With time and patience and commitment from her educators, Alina has accepted different textures, which lets her increasingly engage in collaborative play with other children in the program.

On the opposite end of the spectrum are children who seek constant tactile stimulation, touching furniture, plants, and people. Giving children multiple opportunities to feel different textures can help them regulate the urge to touch. Trays with different textures of sand along with shells, rocks, and corks engage children in pleasurable sensory stimulation. Baskets with different fabrics provide children enough sensory stimulation to keep focused. I enjoy having these baskets in different areas of the classroom, and I bring them out during group gatherings. Setting simple invitations with a limited number of items is ideal for children who are working on decision-making, making sense of their senses, or beginning to explore imaginary worlds. Then children may choose to challenge themselves by incorporating additional Loose Parts.

Finding creative ways to include touch in daily routines can deepen children's ability to engage in play. Start small, experiment to find out what works best, and give yourself and children the gift of time.

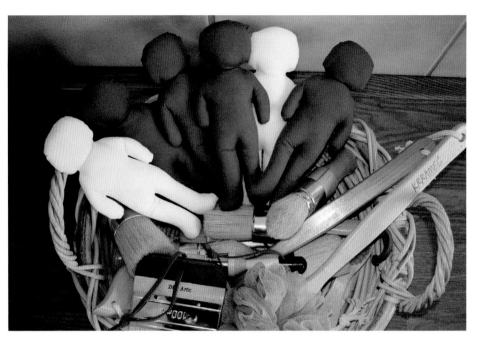

To support a child who is exploring new textures, provide a basket of various types of brushes. Select textures from ultrasoft to very coarse for children to work on sensory sensitivities and develop tactile discrimination skills. Combining the brushes with cloth dolls also develops empathy as children use the brushes to care for their dolls.

Snow invites children with diverse cognitive abilities to create artwork while also developing tactile and temperature awareness. Adding acrylic tubes engages children's interest and piques their curiosity. Children who are developing tolerance for the cold may use scoops or feel the snow through gloves.

Photos: Alexis Baran

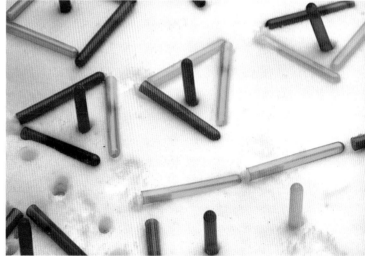

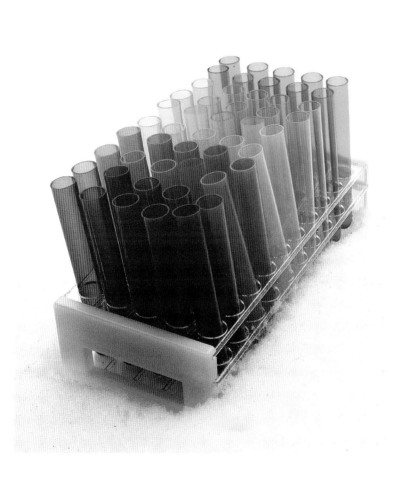

An outdoor mud kitchen with dirt and water for mixing into thicker or thinner substances engages children's imaginations while satisfying a sensory need for children who seek tactile input. This experience also accommodates children who are growing accustomed to messy play or prefer not to touch the dirt directly with their hands—they may use real kitchen tools and utensils to scoop and work with the mud.

An area of softscapes including pillows, blankets, soft woven baskets, and cushions can bring comfort and security to a child who is acclimating to a new space. Felted bowls and place mats can be used to make structures and tell stories.

Photos: Diane Spahn, Director of Education, Kodo Kids

Searching for hard plastic letters in a bowl of water beads is a challenging visual-attention and figure-ground activity that also develops tactile discrimination skills such as stereognosis—the ability to determine objects by touch alone. For children with tactile hypersensitivity, seal water beads in a plastic bag or spread a thin layer of beads on a lipped tray.

Chapter 3
Engaging the Body

The body is an incredibly sophisticated and complex machine. Children's bones and muscles are continually growing, their neurons are constantly connecting, and their senses are perpetually becoming more acute. Let's take a moment to consider how some children with diverse abilities need extra support to help their bodies grow and develop and think about what we can do as educators and family members to ensure that physical accommodations let children engage their bodies to learn. While teaching my college course on diverse abilities and inclusion, I often create experiences for future early childhood educators to explore how physical ability influences learning. Students use tubes as casts to explore not being able to bend their elbows when they need to pick up an object. They tape craft sticks on their fingers to explore what it means not to have full use of their hands. We smear petroleum jelly on plastic eyeglasses to prevent us from seeing clearly. The exploration leads to robust discussions on the importance of supporting the physical development of children with diverse abilities. Together we explore specific accommodations to early childhood ecosystems to ensure full access to the space, materials, and Loose Parts. I highly recommend that educators engage in a similar exploration as they design their physical environments.

When children use their bodies, they also engage in deeper learning. Researchers from the University of Pittsburgh and Carnegie Mellon University considered what happens in the brain as learners progress from novice to expert in certain physical activities. They discovered that new neural activity patterns emerge with long-term learning, and they established a causal link between these patterns and new behavioral abilities. As neuroscientists continue to explore the body-brain connection, they discover that some of the skills and aptitudes children acquire are also mapped onto areas of the brain that control basic body movements. This work helps illuminate neurological connections between the human body, its environment, and the process of learning (Oby et al. 2019).

Another consideration in learning is the strengthening of children's vestibular systems. The vestibular system is in the inner ear, and it regulates movement and our reactions to gravity. It affects balance, bilateral coordination, equilibrium, posture, and muscle tone. It helps us coordinate other senses and affects communication and how we regulate our arousal levels. Using large Loose Parts to balance, walk, jump, and climb on can strengthen the vestibular system, as can tossing beanbags and balls into a basket; dancing with scarves, ribbons, and Hula-Hoops; crawling in and out of a fabric tunnel; rolling in different ways, such as in or on a barrel, tire, or old blanket; sitting on therapy balls instead of chairs; and swinging from a handmade swing.

For decades, early childhood educators have been familiar with the idea that children learn by moving their bodies. In *The Secret of Childhood*, Maria Montessori and Barbara Barclay Carter (2019) highlight the connection between the mind and the body. They argue that movement and physical activity are essential to intellectual growth. Through movement we encounter external reality. Through these contacts, we eventually acquire abstract ideas. In Waldorf education, the concept of eurythmy, the body moving in harmony to rhythm, is central to the curriculum. Eurythmy began as performance art to make music and speech visible. It is another language that allows children to express what they want, need, know, and desire, making their thinking and ideas visible.

Movement, the Body, and Learning

We know that thinking and learning are not all in our head. The body plays a crucial part in our intellectual processes from birth to old age. As our bodies use their senses, we acquire environmental information, which is used to form our understanding of the world. We also express knowledge through our movements, which facilitate greater cognitive function. Our entire brain structure is intimately connected to and strengthened by the movement mechanisms within our bodies. Consider how infants start crawling and how these specific movements help them integrate both hemispheres of the brain, thus strengthening the corpus callosum (the largest connective pathway in the brain, which is made of two hundred million nerve fibers). When both hemispheres are stimulated to coordinate the movement of eyes, hands, feet, and core muscles, cognitive function is strengthened and learning is enhanced (Hannaford 2005).

As infants explore and learn about their bodies and their environment, they engage in all types of movements. They crawl, roll, grasp, throw, sit, fall, totter, and cry for help when needed. This is a time of exploration, discovery, and often just plain fun, as it is filled with wonder and surprise. One of my fondest memories of my oldest daughter is when she was only six months old and she crawled toward the step to the hallway. She placed her hand on the step and attempted to propel her body forward. The first time, she just rolled onto the carpet in the family room. For two weeks, she worked on climbing up that one step. We observed without interfering and gave her the space to work to her goal. It was obvious that she was planning and testing different strategies. Eventually, she managed to climb up, and she turned around with a big smile on her face. That day I learned that there is nothing more extraordinary than observing a child using their body to accomplish what they set out to do. This also made me consider the role the body plays in the development of children and the importance of designing spaces where every child can be successful regardless of physical challenges.

Physical milestones are rooted in movement and the way we use our bodies to explore and make sense of how the world works. Using Loose Parts that allow children to move their bodies supports their development, regardless of ability. Note that development does not progress in a linear fashion. Instead, it occurs in uneven steps or streams of development, and each stage of development opens possibilities for other developmental streams. For instance, Ana did not start to walk until she was two years old. Her fine-motor skills were beyond her developmental stage, but her gross-motor development was slow enough in emerging that her family was concerned and started to assess her for physical disabilities. They enrolled Ana in an inclusive nursery school, and within two weeks of attending the program, Ana started walking. She just needed the time to feel safe separate from her family, and as soon as she was ready, she took off walking and exploring.

Early childhood ecosystems need to offer a variety of sensory integration activities that strengthen children's fine-motor movement, encourage visual motor abilities, increase balance, promote muscle tone, and enhance the proprioceptive and vestibular systems. They also must promote social and emotional development. By knowing the importance of movement, educators can be inspired to design ecosystems that promote movement for all children, including children with diverse abilities.

Movement and Creativity

Widely attributed to Confucius, a common adage reminds us that "I hear and I forget, I see and I remember, I do and I understand." This simple wisdom tells us that we acquire knowledge through engaging the senses and movement. When we use our bodies as we learn, we not only remember but are more deeply engaged in actual learning. Activities like symbolic play, climbing, jumping, running, dancing, skipping, walking, balancing, playing circle games, playing catch, moving to the rhythm of music, engaging in hand-clapping games, playing string games, painting, finger knitting, and many other movement experiences strengthen children's minds and promote learning. We now know that the body is a knowledgeable, conscious, and wise organism that integrates multiple facets of our faculties. We know that when we smell or touch an item, the action helps us retain its image and store it in our memory. In other words, the mind and the body are intricately related and influence each other.

Movement develops and supports our creativity and innovation. My late brother-in-law, artist Byron Galvez, used to paint standing up. I remember watching him and feeling mesmerized by how he used his body to paint large canvases. Think of dancers who use their bodies to communicate their creative thinking and express their emotions in the most beautiful and complex ways. When we observe children in creative flow, we see how their bodies become tools to pursue their ideas. Our creative capacities help us move forward and pursue our ideas and meet our goals. As we move and engage our creative spirit, we are thinking, feeling, and exploring new ways of doing things. Through movement and creativity, we imagine future possibilities, test our ideas and hypotheses, explore new strategies, make mistakes, and embrace a surge of energy and joy in our creative accomplishments.

Children who need extra movement to concentrate benefit from an inclusive environment intentionally planned to accommodate their bodies' needs. For example, Chantelle is in perpetual motion. She sometimes starts building a Loose Parts structure, moves on to another project, but eventually returns to complete what she started. Chantelle uses her body to engage her creativity and just needs adults to understand that she has discovered her own learning process.

Movement and Play

Movement and play go hand in hand. As humans, we have an innate need to play. We play with ideas, which we may call brainstorming. Brainstorming is a playful exchange of knowledge, innovation, creativity, and our profound desire for new discoveries. As we explore new ideas, we gaze out the window, doodle, fidget, pace up and down, open our mouths in amazement, or widen our eyes in recognition of a new finding. The same is true for children. When they are playing, they use their entire bodies. They explore their ideas and discover how they can move in creative ways. For instance, Mathew, who is sometimes challenged to maintain his balance while walking unassisted, consistently practices walking on different surfaces. He creatively places Hula-Hoops and large frames and enjoys jumping and maneuvering his body through the complicated paths he creates. He then transfers the same challenges to smaller explorations, drawing his complicated obstacle courses using paper and markers. He carefully plans and draws mazes on paper, then uses large black cardboard circles to construct them on the floor, testing them by jumping from circle to circle. He has found engaging ways to help him learn to better balance his body.

As children move in play, they become skilled in collaborating with others. Children begin to recognize the strength of their bodies and learn how they can have power over other people. They develop an active sense of how they can be hurt by others and how they themselves can hurt others, growing their awareness of the vulnerability of their bodies and their understanding of who they are within their bodies. In other words, as children gain awareness of how they play with others, they learn that when they are careless or thoughtless, their interactions can result in harm to themselves and others. These are important concepts to learn, and perhaps the only way children can learn these concepts safely is in play.

Equally important is the recognition that a life without movement may lead to stress and mental health issues. I invite you to imagine the price children pay when they sit idle for long stretches of the day, perhaps working on meaningless tasks. Clearly, movement and play come in all sizes and benefit all humans. Movement and play come together in a kinetic and joyful experience. We know that the more children move, the more they learn, just like we know that when children play, they learn.

Movement and Learning

Bending, dancing, jumping, large-body painting and drawing—whatever the form, movement is essential to learning. When children move, they are connecting their vestibular and cerebellar systems, through which they gather sensory information and feedback from the environment. Through movement, children integrate all other sensory systems and increase the levels of oxygen to the brain. As children move, impulses travel back and forth between the cerebellum and other parts of the brain, including the reticular activating system, which regulates the sensory data received. This interaction helps children keep their balance, turn thoughts into action, and coordinate their movements. Play activities that stimulate the inner-ear motion, such as swinging, rolling, jumping, spinning, crawling, skipping, tumbling, and running, are essential to learning. In *Teaching with the Brain in Mind*, Eric Jensen (2005) asserts that many play-oriented movements have the capacity to increase cognition and learning. These activities include active play (chasing, running, and dancing), rough-and-tumble play (wrestling, tug-of-war, and simulated boxing), solitary play (puzzles, Loose Parts play, and object manipulation), and outdoor play (digging, gardening, and observing nature).

Learning through movement is a natural process. When children move, they are learning even without knowing it. This process of implicit learning happens with no labels or specific expectations—yet the impact is profound.

Key Reflections

- What do you notice about how each child in your ecosystem uses their body to move, express themselves, and build relationships?
- What type of provocations, invitations, or inspirations will you offer children to support their motor development and proprioceptive and vestibular system?
- What challenges do you notice that need to be considered as you integrate Loose Parts into the environment to engage children in using their bodies to learn?
- What types of Loose Parts can you infuse into the environment to support the physical development of children with diverse abilities?

The Surprising Stairs

When I visited Wildflower Preschool in Lafayette, Colorado, I placed a new material on the floor in the open block and construction space. The children would be entering the space one by one, allowing for plenty of space to explore the material. They hesitated in approaching it at first but eyed it keenly from the doorway. "What's that thing over there?" asked a curious four-year-old. I encouraged her to take a closer look. "Hey, there's something inside of here," she said. "This thing is made out of wood. Wood is heavy." Another child offered to help with the wooden thing because he could, in his words, handle heavy things. The two set about removing the nesting boxes from their crate and discovered they could be arranged like a staircase. They delighted in moving up and down their structure and made up a lively chant about how feet go up, up, up, and down, down, down. They crawled on the steps and danced on them, too. They wondered out loud if the boxes were strong enough to jump on and looked over at me as if to seek permission. My smile was the answer they sought. The pair quickly arranged the boxes on the floor like islands and took turns jumping up onto and down from each box. Finally, one child proposed a bigger challenge. In hushed voices, they made a plan and announced to me that their design was a surprise. This took several minutes as the boxes were placed in a row with space between each, measured by shoe length. I later learned from the children that "three small shoes or two large shoes with just a teeny tiny bit more" was the perfect amount. For the surprise, they challenged themselves to take big steps to walk only on the boxes and not touch the floor. "Wow!" I exclaimed as both successfully navigated their course.

"We knew we could do it!" one child said.

Another elaborated. "Yep, because there's hot lava underneath!"

—Diane Spahn, Director of Education,
 Kodo Kids

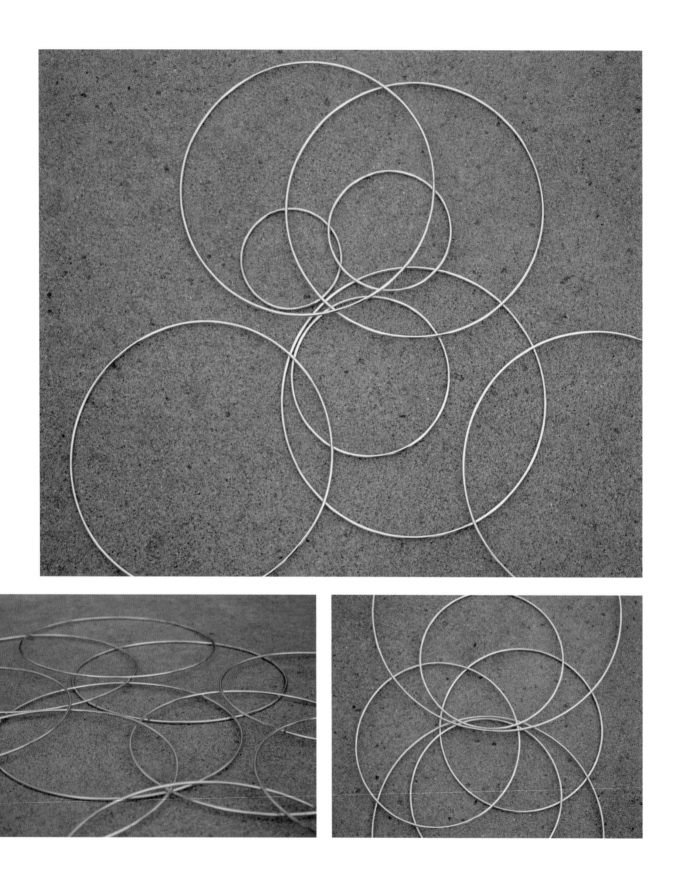

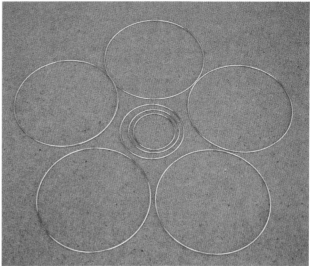

Metal circles encourage gross-motor skills as children design artful arrangements while simultaneously investigating mathematical concepts like seriation and spatial relationships. For children who use a wheelchair or who work best in an upright position, you may offer pegboards on a wall or a large vertical surface such as a fence for arranging or suspending the circles.

Children use their entire bodies to move, climb, and jump on tree stumps. Adjust the size and weight of the stumps to make an appropriate challenge for the children.

Let the children's imagination run wild as they transform logs, branches, and sticks into pretend campfires, hideaway spots, or obstacle courses. Provide handled baskets for gathering the natural materials.

Motor Development

Children use their entire bodies to learn about the world. They learn how things work through perceptual and sensory processes—the steps people take to organize and interpret information. Stop to think about how children perform motor movements. They not only need to acquire control over their muscles, but they must also learn to perceive, anticipate, and respond to the sensory stimuli they discover as they move while holding their bodies stable. Children must also learn to navigate using their perceptions of the spatial arrangement of the environment. Also consider how children use their bodies to manipulate objects. They first need to perceive the form and function of the object. Next, they must understand and predict how an object moves in the surroundings. Children must also distinguish the motion of the object from their bodies movement and the movement of other children. Knowing the complexity of motor development, we can begin to plan how to infuse Loose Parts in the environment to support children's use of their entire bodies.

Contemporary models of therapy and support for children with diverse abilities recognize that all the developmental domains are interconnected and the growth and development of one affects the others. That is why it is crucial to create inclusive environments where children play and learn in the context of relationships and within the boundaries of consistent routines. Such environments support each of the developmental domains. Since this chapter focuses on motor development and how children engage their bodies, we consider how motor development interconnects with other areas of development.

The Connection between Motor and Social Development

Motor development and social development go hand in hand. Think about how children communicate with one another. They gesture, talk, imitate, and guide one another. This requires the ability to understand and physically replicate the movements they see. A devoted system in the brain, the mirror neuron system, helps us perceive and understand other people's actions. For example, when children see a person conduct an activity, such as self-feeding, the mirror neurons create a motor plan for that action in the children's brains. As they develop this movement map, children come to understand the observed actions, motives, and goals and repeat those actions themselves (Woodruff 2018).

The environment and society in which a child lives places specific demands on their motor competencies and physical activities. Factors such as socioeconomic circumstances, geographical location (such as urban or rural), sociocultural factors, and family size all affect children's motor development. For instance, children born early in the year in cold climates will more likely begin to walk during the winter season with snowy terrain outdoors. That simple influence changes the learning experience and also affects how the children learn to maneuver the indoor physical environment. Now consider a child born later in the year. That child will more than likely start walking in the spring or summer and explore the outdoors differently because it will offer them different challenges, surfaces, and terrains to conquer. Sociocultural factors also exert a significant influence on children's motor and social development. When children live in a society in which spontaneous, informal, playful, and physically active behaviors are encouraged, their gross-motor development, such as jumping and running, increases. When children live in a society that promotes quiet activity such as drawing, manipulating small objects, and writing, fine-motor skills increase (Venetsanou and Kambas 2009).

Playing collaboratively depends on the connections between motor and social development. Designing ecosystems where children interact with one another and engage with Loose Parts promotes the use of their bodies while they engage socially. For instance, three-year-old Josiah has limited use of his right hand. Tossing a ball presents a challenge, so he prefers other activities when he plays outdoors. The educators have noticed how Josiah watches as other children play catch or toss balls into empty large frames. They want Josiah to join in more collaborative play. With that goal in mind, they invite all the children to talk about other Loose Parts they can practice tossing and catching. The children share a variety of ideas; they think beanbags would be fun and easier to catch. They consider the idea of threading a rope through an Oball to guide the ball's direction during tossing and catching. Josiah is particularly engaged and enthusiastic. He is willing to try out any plan, and he feels like he belongs and can be part of the collaborative process. For weeks the children test new items to throw and containers to catch the Loose Parts. They keep a chart and ask the educators to keep track of which Loose Parts are easier for Josiah to throw. This story shows how children can benefit from being part of an inclusive environment where Loose Parts have been carefully infused.

The Connection between Motor and Cognitive Development

Development and learning occur through dynamic interactions with the physical environment and the social world. In recent years, increasing attention has been paid to the contributions of a healthy and well-functioning motor system for children's learning. Consequently, it seems evident that motor development is critical for children's understanding of the physical and social world (Libertus and Hauf 2017). When children develop gross-motor skills such as walking, running, and jumping, they are also developing their cognitive abilities. This is because the cerebellum, which is the main region of the brain responsible for motor skills, is also connected to visual processing, spatial perception, and cognitive ability. When children use their brains to engage in physical movement, they are developing the same neural pathways that serve cognitive activity. Let's not forget that movement, particularly active and exuberant movement, brings more oxygen, water, and glucose to the brain to support both physical and cognitive ability.

Cognition and physical development are interconnected. Infants demonstrate innate reflexes at birth, yet many of their movements are purposeful and intentional. When they discover control over their hands, they can begin to grasp, hold, and pick up objects. Eventually, every movement is planned and coordinated. Anticipating the outcomes of movements promotes cognitive development. When we observe Genaro, who is working on strengthening his fine-motor skills, we notice that he thoughtfully uses a dropper to fill an ice cube tray with colorful water. We can see his concentration and we can almost read the thinking process taking place. His physical and cognitive development are not disembodied processes. The body does more than carry the brain from place to place—our entire brain structure is intimately connected to and grown by the movement mechanisms within our bodies. Our bodies' senses feed our brains environmental information, which forms our understanding of the world, and we draw from this information when creating new possibilities (Hannaford 2005).

Children need healthy, harmonious, and engaging noncompetitive movement activities to develop their brains. The movement of their bodies and their love for learning create the pathways in their minds for reading, writing, spelling, and mathematical and creative thinking (Johnson n.d.). Children love creating obstacle courses using large Loose Parts such as wooden planks, tree stumps, milk crates, river rocks, large frames, Hula-Hoops, and large drainage tubes. Through such gross-motor play, they understand moving over, under, around, through, beside, and near objects as well as other mathematical, language, and literacy concepts.

The Connection between Motor and Emotional Development

Educators recognize that emotions and feelings affect children's performance and learning, and so does the state of the body, such as how well a child has slept and eaten. But the relationship between learning, emotion, and the use of our bodies runs much deeper than we may realize. Children's ability to move their bodies is closely related to the way they feel about their success and agency. Connections between motor and emotional development help children recognize their own capacities and how they use their bodies in risk-taking. When children learn to trust their bodies as part of learning and exploring, they develop a strong sense of self. They know what they can and cannot do. They acquire a sense of space and a strong safety compass. In the words of Howard Gardner, "I want my children to understand the world, but not just because the world is fascinating and the human mind is curious. I want them to understand it so that they will be positioned to make it a better place. . . . An important part of that understanding is knowing who we are and what we can do" (1999, 180–81). Gardner's theory of multiple intelligences argues why it is important to include different ways of moving and thinking to support children's growth and development.

Throwing lightweight ball pit balls into rings is a total-body movement activity for muscle strengthening and can help children who are starting to develop motor planning and coordination skills like eye-hand coordination. Ensure that the container of balls is placed in an accessible location and height for a child using a wheelchair, stander, or other mobility device. Use a slingshot or other methods of aiming and throwing the lightweight balls to adapt this task for children with varied upper extremity mobility.

Scooping, digging, piling, and molding snow using cups, plates, and hands engages children's core muscles and extremities to develop whole-body strength while promoting bilateral skills.

Photos: Alexis Baran

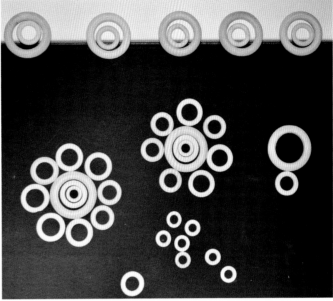

The tiny size of these natural maple circles encourages fine-motor precision and in-hand manipulation as children carefully place the pieces using their fingertips, stacking them on top of each other, lining them up, or making endless patterns and designs.

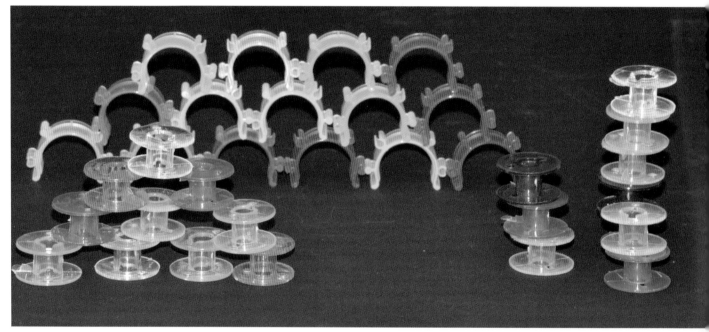

Add a new challenge for children with advanced fine-motor abilities. These lightweight plastic bobbins and accessories require great precision to manipulate and balance.

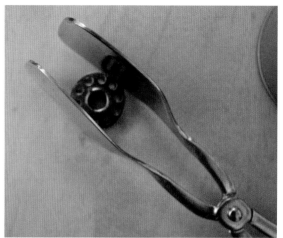

Grasping and transferring items using tongs (regular or scissor type) support motor learning and prepare children for related skills like cutting with scissors. For children beginning to use their fingers rather than palms to grasp tools and drawing implements, opt for wider transfer containers to increase motivation and success.

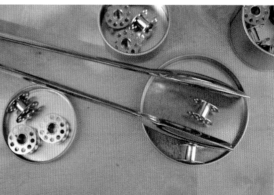

The Proprioceptive and Vestibular Systems

We often consider only five senses: sight, smell, sound, taste, and touch. I have memories of studying each of these senses in school with no mention of the next two essential senses—the proprioceptive and the vestibular—that coordinate and position our bodies as we walk, run, jump, dance, and learn through movement. How we move is determined by the signals our bodies receive from our surroundings. Our bodies are powerful and incredible machines, and we don't often stop to think about how they work. I remember that as a child I had a profound desire to be a dancer. I loved to move, explore how my body worked, and work out how to do complicated twists and turns. I remember moments when I got lost in the music and rhythm and allowed my muscles to guide me. I did not recognize how my proprioceptive sense was taking over or know that I kept my balance through my vestibular sense.

Our arms, legs, and trunks respond to sensations from both the proprioceptive and vestibular systems. The proprioceptive sense perceives the amount of force against the body. Proprioceptive input to the muscles and joints is regulating, and it can be either calming or alerting. Holding hands or giving hugs is uncomfortable for some children who will do anything to avoid pressure or movement of the body. The information proprioception provides us allows us to maneuver our way around obstacles in the dark or through a space. The proprioceptive system also helps us manipulate Loose Parts and other objects. The ability to sense our bodies is critical for telling us where we are in relation to our surroundings as well as being able to execute specific movements to solve everyday problems (Proske and Gandevia 2016).

The vestibular system, also known as our balance center, is responsible for receiving information regarding how our bodies move in space as well as acceleration and deceleration. The receptors in this system in the inner ear are stimulated by changes in head position. The vestibular system keeps us from falling and helps us retain our balance.

Try this exercise to help you understand how the proprioceptive and vestibular senses work together. Find another adult to help you. Stand with your eyes closed and extend both arms in front of you. You may not see them, but you know that they are there. Now your partner can add a five-pound weight to each hand. Your eyes are still closed, but suddenly there is a different sensation in your arms. The extra weight either makes you tired or shifts your energy. Add another five pounds per arm, and how will that increase or decrease your tolerance? Does it change your body awareness? Do you want to drop the weights or keep holding them? At a certain point, you will either let go of the weights or shift the position of your arms. As you may have noticed, it requires a lot of thinking and using specific strategies to respond and control the messages coming from your hands as the weight increases. But what happens when the signals are not strong enough or are too strong? The dysregulation causes bumping, crashing, climbing, and falling. Children may need to be continually moving or choose to sit and watch on the sidelines. They may exert too much pressure when painting or drawing to the point of breaking pencils or brushes or may refuse to engage in many art explorations. They may misjudge the distance and force needed when picking up Loose Parts, thus spilling or sending the items rolling. They may be exuberant and active or avoid any type of physical exertion.

An ecosystem that promotes equity and inclusion must meet the vestibular and proprioceptive needs of all children. Begin by observing the way children move in the space. Four-year-old Samuel always participates during storytelling, singing, and dancing. He uses his entire body and enthusiastically encourages other children to join. The minute that children are asked to sit to listen to directions or talk to one another, Samuel starts to wiggle and attempts to leave the circle. Outdoors he runs, jumps, and arranges large Loose Parts to create complex obstacle courses. He fills the wagon with heavy tree stumps and river rocks and uses his entire body to move it around the yard. He stacks heavy tires on top of each other, climbing on the first tire to propel the next tire up to the top. He works hard, and when it is time to rest, he easily falls asleep. But the minute he wakes up, he walks to find the cove crown molding in the construction area and begins to create ramps to explore the trajectory of cars and balls. He works on his ramps until it is time to go home. Then there is three-year-old Alondra, who watches and walks around the room. She prefers quieter explorations and often sits on a pillow, sorting colorful mini tubes or filling small Mylar bags with a variety of beads. She opens and closes the bags until she is satisfied they are full enough. When children invite her to join in more physical activities, she just walks away. Outdoors she sometimes goes to the swing but always keeps her feet on the ground. She does not join in moving the large Loose Parts and prefers to construct small fairy worlds using silk petals, colorful pebbles, bamboo sticks, tree cookies, and mini tree stumps. During circle time, she actively participates but prefers to stand to the side when movement activities are taking place.

Strong proprioceptive and vestibular processing is fundamental in building a child's sense of self and in achieving important developmental milestones. It is crucial to create ecosystems that both promote and respect the children's proprioceptive and vestibular systems with Loose Parts, tools, and materials:

- large tubes where children can sit or lay on their tummies to roll back and forth
- tree stumps in the outdoor area to push themselves up
- toilet plungers and a bucket with paint to paint on butcher paper
- bricks in the outdoor area to build and engage in heavy lifting
- bubbles to blow, encouraging scientific thinking while also strengthening oral and facial muscles

Dancing ribbons encourage children to move their bodies in new ways, facilitating proprioception as well as body and spatial awareness. Add soft foam tubing to build up the handle or use an adaptive cuff to aid children in grasping the ribbon wand.

Large Loose Parts like tree stumps or heavy branches let children practice balancing and engaging their full bodies. Their proprioception is particularly engaged when they push, climb on, roll, and move the large items to make obstacle courses.

Bending, digging, pushing, and balancing the body in the sand while attaching scarves to balloon holders encourages children's fine-motor skills. For children not yet ready for the fine-motor component, tossing and catching the scarves engages proprioception and body awareness.

Stretchy silicone fidgets engage proprioception through resistance and pull on bones and joints. They serve as Loose Parts in dramatic play as well as self-regulating, coping, or attentional tools for children with neurodiversity or any child who benefits from tactile fidget breaks.

Children can incorporate different walking surfaces into their self-made gross-motor obstacle courses. For children who use a wheelchair or walker, place surfaces on a tabletop so they can explore the textures and sensations with their hands.

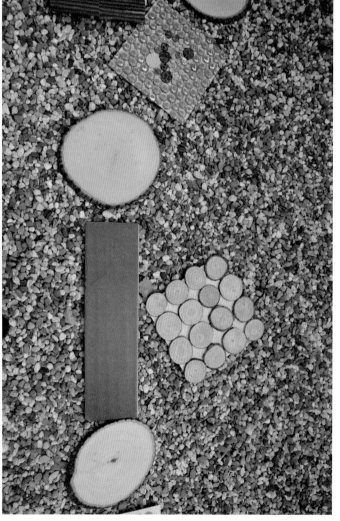

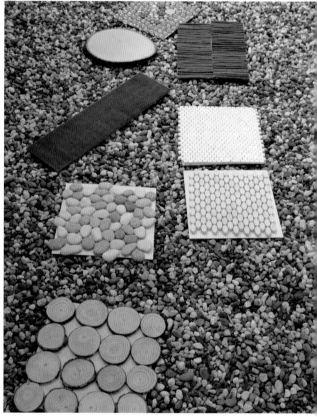

Body Strength and Stability

During my time as an educator, I have noticed a trend of children struggling with coordinated movement. We see that they trip and fall more often when walking on different surfaces, or they bump into furniture and one another. I also have noticed how they lean the top portion of the body on a table for support while they attempt to write or how they hold one hand with the other hand when writing. Many children lack the strength to hang from the monkey bars or climb a play structure with confidence. As educators, we must create ecosystems where children can move, challenge their bodies, and take risks that strengthen their bodies to help them thrive, grow, and learn.

We strengthen children's bodies by following their innate curiosity to learn and know how the world functions. For example, infants crawl to an item that interests them, pick it up, and joyfully explore it with their hands—or mouth! This simple movement requires strength and coordination. Infants must balance their bodies to come to a crawling position. Their core and other muscles must be strong enough to hold the position and move their arms and legs in unison. As they pick up an object, they need to coordinate their fine-motor skills and learn to use their fingers and hands together. Now, imagine the strength that is required as the infants propel themselves to a standing position. Curiosity and interest in exploring push them to move and strengthen their bodies, from infancy into childhood.

Building Core Strength

Core strength includes the outer core, or the abdominals, and the inner core, or the muscles surrounding the hips, pelvic floor, diaphragm, and spine.

Core strength might bring to mind a six-pack sculpted torso. But a strong inner core offers stability for the spine and allows for proper alignment and smooth, coordinated movement. The inner core supports our posture, activates the diaphragm and helps us establish breathing patterns, and provides a strong base from which the outer core muscles can move. When children's inner cores are strong, they can stand upright with stability. Children with limited inner cores strength often present with a slumped posture, decreased endurance, and poor balance. When children don't have good inner core strength, they compensate by using the more superficial outer core muscles to keep their bodies upright, which can interfere with overall development (Hanscom 2016). Outer core muscles support pushing and pulling actions, such as climbing a tree or pushing or pulling a wagon to transport items from one end of the yard to the other. Engaging the outer core muscles requires more energy and concentration. When children's outer cores are weak, they may give up too fast on a more strenuous activity.

There is nothing better than play, especially outdoor play, to promote core strength. The outdoors encourages strength development as it provides children with a changing environment. Many activities require the inner and outer core to provide stability and mobility as children adjust their bodies to accommodate complex movement. Children develop both inner and outer core strength when they walk on a fallen tree branch, jump along a series of wooden circles, or dig in the sandbox. A ray of sun or reflected rainbow on the floor prompts a crawler to scoot from the shade to reach it. A grassy slope encourages children to roll down or make a race for the top. These movements engage the large-muscle groups in varied ways and build a strong base of support that improves posture and allows the arms, legs, head, and eyes to move around and function better, leading to better looking and listening (Hanscom 2016). When children have a typical development process, core activation and postural control happen naturally and smoothly.

Movement is dynamic and essential to children's well-being. When children play and are given adequate space and ample time to move, they grow strong and healthy from the physical activity. When children have strong core muscles, their spines are protected from damage and pain, and the core muscles help them use their arms and legs powerfully and effectively. At the same time, we must recognize that some children have mobility needs or avoid sensory stimulation, and we must make adaptations to support their physical activity needs.

Using the Body to Communicate

In previous chapters, I mentioned how all areas of development are integrated. Children's curiosity and interest in making sense of the world (cognitive development) support movement (physical development). They turn when they see light coming through the window or when they hear someone's voice (physical development senses). When they dance, play, and move with other children (social development), they develop muscle strength. As children turn or reach out to be picked up when they need comforting (emotional development), they strengthen their core muscles and develop a stable trunk. The more children move and explore using their bodies in various ways, the more their musculoskeletal, sensory, and motor-control systems work together for smooth, coordinated functional movement.

Now let's consider children who have limited inner or outer muscle strength and what we can do to support them. Children who have not developed typical muscle strength and have low muscle tone may lack the strength or endurance to maintain good posture and other physical alignments, which limits how they activate the core muscles. Children who have challenges with sensory processing may also have low muscle strength. They may not process vestibular sensory input, which impacts their perception of the alignment and use of their muscles. Notice how some children hold their breath to compensate when they have difficulty with core muscle functioning. Often children create a unique set of compensations to gain central stability, such as holding their hands tight to their sides to obtain trunk symmetry. These compensations may interfere with the development of necessary skills. Observing and documenting what you see is crucial to offering extra support as children need it.

A body's overall muscle tone, or the amount of tension a muscle has at rest, also supports body movement and body posture. Early in my career, I worked with young children who experienced hypertonicity, or high muscle tone or tension. Their muscles contracted frequently, and I helped them relax their muscles by using engaging toys and materials. Imagine if you had a cast around your knee and someone tried to bend it. Not only is it impossible, but it can create irreversible harm. Being gentle and creating opportunities to relax and move at their own pace is helpful for children with hypertonicity. Rocking, gentle swinging, pushing baskets, and pulling tubes attached to strings helps children relax. Using massage rollers, gently tickling with feathers, and placing Loose Parts at arm's length to encourage stretching may also help children to relax enough to move their muscles more effectively.

The opposite of hypertonicity is hypotonicity, a condition characterized by decreased tone or tension. Provide different surfaces for children to crawl or walk on to create varied levels of resistance. Make obstacle courses with pillows and cushions of different sizes to strengthen the muscles. Take, for example, Soraya, who is three years old and has low upper muscle strength. She enjoys climbing up and down ramps and has been working hard to strengthen her arms and torso. Educators added a rope to the outdoor slide to help her climb up the slide, which she does often. Her occupational therapist follows her up the slide and watches closely. When Soraya gets on top of the slide, she sits and looks around, notices a basket with balls, picks them up, and starts throwing them down the slide. Joshua notices the balls coming down, and he begins to pick them up. Other children join in, and a game of toss and catch begins. To encourage Soraya to engage in bilateral play, the therapist hands Soraya the balls from her right and left sides. This prompts Soraya to turn and get the balls while crossing the midline. Soraya is strengthening her muscles while developing social skills as she plays with other children.

Children can create their own jumping games using jump circles. Children who are developing body strength and balance or who seek added sensory input can jump with their arms and legs (frog jumps) and increase stability.

Building with blocks of various weights challenges children to use their bodies while being inclusive of children with diverse body abilities.

Photos: Diane Spahn, Director of Education, Kodo Kids

Using clothespins of different sizes builds fine-motor strength. Adjust the size and tension of the pins so a child can be successful, or wrap a rubber band around the end to help them maintain their grasp.

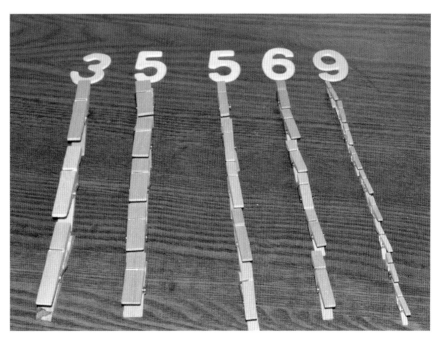

Incorporate bulky recycled Loose Parts like large crates, film reels, and gutters to build upper-body strength and stability. Moving such large items encourages teamwork.

Large wooden arches and circles, wooden figures, and blocks all engage the body as children crouch, bend, reach, and move around the outdoor circular workspace. During ground-level play, place a wedge support or other firm cushion under the chest to help children who are building core and upper-body strength, providing them with the stability needed to reach for items.

Chapter 4
Engaging the Brain

Infants and young children live in a sensory world: they touch, feel, smell, and listen. They use their entire bodies to move and explore, then process the information they receive through their senses. The act of processing new knowledge and information as it is acquired is cognition, and it is the way we make meaning of what is going on in the world, seeing patterns and creating connections between experiences. Engaging the brain in this way promotes the development of executive functions, otherwise known as the management system of the brain. Executive functions allow us to accomplish goals, perform tasks, make plans, and get things done—influencing almost every aspect of our lives.

Infants begin to make connections to the Loose Parts they touch; when a soft sponge feels pleasurable, they recognize it and will select it from other rougher items. When they recognize a familiar voice, they smile and laugh in response. Before infants can use the word *sponge* (for a Loose Part) or *mommy* (for a familiar voice), they make a link to the pleasing sensation, and they create rudimentary mental patterns that help them place experiences into categories that guide their thinking and cognitive processing. As children grow, their cognitive processing skills become much more elaborate. They begin to use their experiences and understanding of how things work to form complex schemas, which lead to manipulating more abstract ideas. They now know that a Loose Part still exists even when it is not in front of them. They use their creativity and put different abstract ideas together, dream up imaginary worlds, and explore possibilities for the future as they integrate their past ideas and learning. Thus they acquire cognitive skills that help them interact with the world.

One reason children with diverse abilities have trouble with cognitive processing is that it relies on sensory input, which may be lacking, confusing, or overwhelming. Perhaps as it is perceived through the senses, the signal lacks a recognizable pattern they can process and decipher.

Core Cognitive Skills

Our brains' cognitive skills let us think, learn, remember, self-regulate, reason, and pay attention. The core cognitive skills work together to help children take in information from the environment and store the knowledge they use every day to function in society.

Building Sustained Attention

From my years of experience and observation of children engaged in Loose Parts play, I have noticed that Loose Parts may be crucial in creating neural networks in the brains of very young children. Not only do Loose Parts stimulate the senses, but they also support children in identifying specific features that capture their attention, help them focus, and sustain their attention. These early skills are the foundation of later learning. Sustained attention relates to the ability to stay focused on a task for long periods. When children are surrounded by positive affect or emotions, encouraging responses, and interesting explorations, they are more likely to demonstrate sustained attention. When children have a variety of engaging and stimulating Loose Parts, they continue discovering and maintaining focus for longer periods, and their ability to concentrate, identify features in items, and make connections between the different items grows. Without sustained attention, new learning simply does not happen.

Creative Cognition

The theory of Loose Parts is founded on the belief that these open-ended materials promote children's creativity. The possibilities and limitations of Loose Parts combined with children's understanding of what they can do with the materials and what they can think and do as learners develops children's creative cognition. Creative cognition concerns how cognitive processes help us use past experiences and knowledge to yield new ideas to complete a task or solve a problem. According to Robert J. Sternberg (2018), professor of human development at Cornell University, being creative is the ability to defy common thinking and our beliefs and values. Until we defy our thinking, ideas, and beliefs to challenge what society imposes on us, we can't be creative. What an opportunity we have to help children defy their own capacities and ideas! Loose Parts help children go beyond what they think and expect of themselves to a more accepting, nonjudgmental way of being that ensures creativity and success.

Children with diverse abilities need opportunities to develop creative thinking, and Loose Parts allow them to express their ideas and thinking in creative ways. They are in charge of what they do and how they use the materials. They gain understanding and explore possibilities with success. They also make necessary mistakes and find alternate solutions to what they are pursuing. Children with diverse abilities can have the freedom to attribute different Loose Parts with functions and meanings that speak to them. They can use their imaginations to create scenes that represent what they know and what they understand, which is central to meaning making and sense making.

Cognitive Flexibility

Humans, including children, have the right and ability to change their minds. Cognitive flexibility is the ability to change our thinking and adapt to a new situation or a new environment, allowing us to abandon strategies that are no longer helpful in accomplishing a specific task and then focus our energy on new and more promising ways to solve a problem (Kaufman and Sternberg 2019). Cognitive flexibility is required every day as we find ways to maneuver new challenges. When children with diverse abilities build with blocks, tree cookies, and tree trunks, they use cognitive flexibility as they decide which blocks to use to create a stabler structure. Loose Parts promote a range of cognitively complex play experiences that allow children to shift their thinking and adapt to new situations. An acrylic tube can be used on the light table to explore colors and transparency, and it can also be filled with water in the water table. Loose Parts inject novelty into children's play, thus sustaining their interest. Children shift mental gears from one idea to another, and they are open to testing their thinking because there is no sense of failure.

The open-ended properties of Loose Parts support children's understanding of their own learning capabilities. For example, children decide how they can move, manipulate, and combine mini pine cones, seeds, pebbles, and stones to make sculptures, use as pretend money, or "cook" into a soup, thus developing higher levels of critical thinking and cognitive flexibility by making choices and connecting the items to actual experiences. This work lets children test their abilities and learn what they are capable of accomplishing.

When children begin to read, flexible thinking helps them understand how letters combine into different configurations to create words and how words can be used in more than one way. Flexible thinking helps us focus our attention on what is important when we study or follow the plot and characters in an exciting story. Flexible thinking lets us prioritize important tasks and decide which tasks can wait. We truly use cognitive flexibility every minute of the day.

Cognitive Control

In Loose Parts play, children with diverse abilities gain confidence and are more open to making mistakes and mentally shifting to explore new perspectives. They can respond to plans and goals set by themselves, peers, or adults. As children grow and learn new concepts and skills, they need to explore them in multiple ways. They can plan how they will use Loose Parts in different areas of the ecosystem and on different surfaces. Educators and families support children by giving verbal meaning to children's ideas and guiding them to plan and meet their goals. For example, "Emma, I see that you planned to balance the tree stumps on top of the block tower. I also noticed that you balanced the rocks on top of one another. Let's look at the photos we took to see if they help you meet your goal." Using photographs and narratives helps children apply new concepts in different contexts and strengthen their plans so they can meet their goals.

Part of cognitive control concerns the ability to transition from one activity to the next. Children with diverse abilities, along with all children, benefit from smooth transitions. Let children know what every part of the day looks like and give them regular updates to help them mentally prepare to move from one part of the schedule to the next. Of course, it is most effective to provide significant uninterrupted blocks of time for play.

Working Memory

The working memory system combines cognitive activities such as reasoning, learning, and comprehension. It is the ability to hold on to information without losing track of what we are doing. Think of working memory as a sticky note you temporarily place in your brain. It has the new information you need to connect to other information that helps you complete a task. Working memory affects both short- and long-term memory. Being able to focus and pay attention is helpful to develop working memory. For example, when five-year-old Sahara selects marbles to make patterns, she sorts them by color, size, and material. She uses her memory to categorize each marble and choose the next one in her patterns. Sahara struggles with processing a lot of information all at once. This type of Loose Parts play helps her develop both her focus and her working memory, aiding the brain in organizing information so that Sahara can apply the information to similar situations and categorize other types of Loose Parts.

Planning

The mental process of planning allows us to organize specific actions to reach a goal, decide the priority of the steps we need to take to meet that goal, and consider the resources we need to accomplish it (Morris and Ward 2005). Planning stimulates the brain to generate and evaluate possible solutions to a problem. It allows us to explore possibilities. For example, having a clear understanding of the current state of a sequence of imaginative play can guide children to the next sequence in the story they are creating. As children test how Loose Parts sink or float, they practice problem-solving skills and strategies. By planning and deeply thinking about the affordances of different Loose Parts, they can more efficiently and systematically explore every possibility and determine how to further test their hypotheses.

Planning includes the ability to mentally visualize or make a mental representation of the problem, including the specific steps, ideas, and actions to take. Planning can also start with a goal in mind as we trace the steps backward to identify challenges and opportunities and make changes to improve the outcome. Loose Parts have often been identified in conjunction with heuristic explorations—that is, supporting children to discover or learn something for themselves through trial and error. The heuristic approach requires children to make plans as they select Loose Parts they can manipulate, interact with, and create with.

Loose Parts stimulate executive function and promote cognitive skills and abilities as children think about how and when to use the materials. They can move the Loose Parts and combine them with other materials to create multiple meanings and apply their understanding of the affordances of the Loose Parts. Children with diverse abilities benefit from ongoing open-ended exploration and using Loose Parts to build, construct, wonder, use their curiosity, and engage in mathematical and scientific thinking.

Key Reflections

- How can you organize Loose Parts, tools, and materials so that children can easily identify and access them?
- What type of opportunities can you offer children with diverse abilities to explore and test their ideas?
- How will you rearrange your daily schedule to give children time to practice new skills until they develop a sense of mastery?

Magnets and Rings

Bryson was engaged in a project using magnet tiles. He built a tower and counted how many stories high it was. He then walked over to the shelf and retrieved the container of metal rings. Bryson started to stack the metal rings next to the magnet tile tower he built. Bryson used the rings to represent the number of stories he had previously counted in the tower. He made the stack starting at one and increased it to four metal rings tall. Bryson compared the quantities to one another. He cheered with joy when the quantities matched. Bryson excitedly exclaimed, "They're the same! Look—one, two, three, four. And look—one, two, three, four. They are the same. See!" After Bryson was satisfied with his increasing quantities of metal rings, he placed his hand flat on top to show a physical connection of equal heights. He turned to me with a smile of strong self-confidence and the awareness of having learned something new.

—Debbie McMannis, Lincoln Community Preschool

Baskets filled with real-life and multisensory items captivate children's natural curiosity and stimulate the senses, strengthening cognitive development. Swap out items to find things the children are particularly drawn to exploring.

Children use critical-thinking and problem-solving skills to balance and stack real rocks, making tall towers and structures. For children with lower muscle tone or endurance, offer thinner or lighter rocks or wooden or plastic Loose Parts.

Children make beautiful designs and use their executive-functioning skills when they collect, sort, and classify natural Loose Parts.

Motivation and Engagement

Children nowadays contend with so many prospects competing for their attention and engagement—media, peer groups, organized activities, and more. We know that motivation is a drive, the inner force that keeps children going and mastering challenging tasks. To maintain their motivation and engagement, they need adults to create environments that support their interests and place their ideas at the center of learning. Furthermore, being motivated helps children find that spark for life—so they wish to be successful because they genuinely want to and not because they are receiving an external reward or praise. E. Paul Torrance (1993a), an expert on creativity, designed a framework that focuses on creative thinking, motivation, and engagement. He proposed three stages (heighten anticipation, deepen expectation, extend the learning) that increase motivation and keep a person's interest going so they dig deeper and discover new ideas and solutions. The Torrance framework requires us to defer judgment, making use of all the senses, opening new doors, and targeting problems to be considered or solutions to be incorporated into daily life.

Nothing motivates and engages children more than play that they initiate and maintain without adult intervention or guidance. Children have individual and unique motivators based on their strengths, perceptions, and ability to complete a task. What one child finds motivating will differ from another. Some children are skillful builders, while other children enjoy music or painting. The educator's role is to observe what motivates individual children and create play opportunities that support their strengths, ideas, and interests. Learning what keeps individual children motivated and engaged may seem like a daunting job for educators and families. However, remember that the best motivator is play. Because Loose Parts offer multiple affordances, children use them in their own way. With that simple knowledge, educators can turn their efforts to scaffolding, challenging, and further responding to children's interests and ideas.

Create a culture where mistakes are celebrated and recognized as the way children enter the learning process, rather than seen as failing to meet a standard. Accepting mistakes is particularly essential for children with diverse abilities, who may take longer to comprehend and adapt to new ideas and concepts. To keep children motivated, educators must preserve children's self-esteem and their self-concept as successful learners. The open-ended qualities of Loose Parts give children the ability to create challenges but not feel like they must give an answer or respond to please the educator. Instead, Loose Parts children celebrate their successes! Making choices from the many play possibilities available encourages regulation skills and helps children learn how to make choices. When children with diverse abilities follow their interests, they become more involved and more willing to participate in the classroom community. They engage in a greater variety of activities, explorations, and social and physical play, which can lead to more complex verbal and nonverbal communication.

Engagement is the key to success for children with diverse abilities, and they need individualized challenges that keep them engaged and motivated. The Loose Parts philosophy is rooted in the belief that it puts children in charge of their play and learning. The more they play and explore the affordances of Loose Parts, the more they want to continue. Creativity brings fun, joy, and success, improving outcomes for all children. With this knowledge in mind, curate Loose Parts to present challenges that keep children motivated and engaged. Observe how children use Loose Parts and how frequently. As you notice motivation and engagement slowing, create a provocation that encourages children to think differently. For example, provide different types of blocks, such as tree stumps, Tumi Ishi balancing blocks, unit blocks, corrugated blocks, KAPLA blocks, or Dr. Drew's Blocks to create interest and challenge children to play differently. Blocks are essential in inclusive and equitable ecosystems. Playing with blocks helps children develop important skills such as problem solving, perspective taking, and executive functioning.

Challenges that connect children's sensory processing and motor planning to their feelings and emotions increase their engagement and motivation. Symbolic or dramatic play supports children in expressing their feelings and ideas. Loose Parts used in storytelling motivate children to communicate their thinking. Combining Loose Parts with more concrete objects, such as felt animals, supports children's ability to go from concrete to symbolic representation as they re-create dramatic play sequences from their imagination and experiences. Begin by creating simple play worlds with Loose Parts and work toward engaging children in more complex play sequences.

Invite children to take initiative and experience joy in solving a problem. When a child enjoys creating works of art using feathers or designing with glass beads, make these materials readily available and add other Loose Parts to create more complex designs. When children are interested in what they are doing, they gain a sense of mastery, develop their creativity, and increase their self-confidence.

As an educator, you hold a lot of power to engage and motivate children. Your presence is crucial. Build deep connections with children by observing, responding, and having a genuine interest in what they say and do and how they act. Focus on their strengths rather than just meeting their needs. Children will know that you care and that they can trust you to guide them. As you observe children playing with Loose Parts, strengthen as many of the children's basic developmental capacities as you can, including the ability to be more engaged and more motivated to complete a task. In other words, notice their attention, focus, engagement, nonverbal gestural interactions, use of symbols and words, and back-and-forth dialogues, including fantasies and imaginative play (Greenspan, Wieder, and Simons 1998). As much as possible, create experiences that build relationships and encourage interactions, because they also increase engagement and motivation. If an experience initially involves little interaction, take the experience's essence and re-create it in a more collaborative approach. For example, when a child shows interest in weaving with colorful ribbons, create a collaborative weaving space.

Engagement and motivation require trying new things and making decisions. Positive risk-taking emphasizes managing risk, not ignoring it, and it involves developing strategies so the risks of an activity are balanced against the benefits. Educators need to assess their own risk compass and create ecosystems that protect against hazards but allow children to take risks. This process requires reflection and creativity in terms of how educators perceive and reframe risk-taking. It also requires acknowledging how this can be stressful for adults. Making a significant change in practice requires educators, programs, and agencies to respond to their individual and collective concerns and develop long-term, successful, positive risk-taking practices. The hope is that when we weigh the positive effects of positive risk-taking, educators will be ready to infuse Loose Parts and stand back to allow children to explore them freely, even when it is outside the adults' comfort zones.

Children need to relax and reflect to allow their bodies to catch up with their brains. When they slow down, they are able to stay more focused and are more motivated to achieve their goals. Strive to create balance in the classroom ecosystem. Ensure that there is enough sensory stimulation as well as quiet places to retreat when children need time to reflect and regulate. Add Loose Parts that provide sensory experiences, such as transparent and colorful cake-pop sticks that children can explore at the light table. Offer Oballs and sensory balls with different textures. Place small blocks in the reading area for an extra sensory exploration that can help children retain focus. Provide fidgets throughout the ecosystem for self-regulating. Soft pillows and warm weighted blankets provide comfort. Sand play has a powerful calming effect on children. Incorporate Jurassic Sands or similar play sand, beach sand, and sand that has a variety of textures. Add driftwood, coconut shells, seedpods, and pine cones to the sand to increase the sensory value. My mother always talked about the calming effects of water. She told me that listening to and looking at the water helps heal you. A small water fountain in the classroom brings calming sounds, and a water table with warm water is a welcome exploration. Add acrylic tubes of different sizes—children hear the sound and watch intently as they transfer water from one tube to the other. Water beads in small containers give children much-needed relaxation. Include acrylic letters or silicone beads to increase interest and engagement.

As I researched this book, I was not surprised to see an overwhelming consensus that you must use a behavioral intervention system based on rewards and consequences to keep children with diverse abilities engaged and compliant. These recommended practices do not seem inclusive, respectful, or supportive to me. I want to shift the paradigm to a more benign and inclusive understanding of children with diverse abilities. Let's focus on children's inner capacities as the sole motivator and play as the best reward we can give children. When the classroom ecosystem is infused with alluring and novel Loose Parts, children will spend a lot of time on what interests them. They feel motivated to test, change, and improve on the goals they establish for themselves.

Children of diverse physical, mental, and sensory capacities can insert colorful corrugated circle cutouts into repurposed tissue boxes. The lightweight materials assist with the task, and the textured paper surface engages them to manipulate, sort, and insert the pieces.

Wooden half circles can create many complex designs. Children with high-level executive functioning and exceptional design skills may expand their learning by combining these with additional constructive Loose Parts.

Photos: Kasey Kile, Director of Professional Development, Kodo Kids

Scent is motivating for many children. Cedar blocks and cinnamon sticks offer safe, natural smells. Observe children during play to ensure the scent is not overstimulating.

Young children are curious about the physical characteristics of objects and how they can combine with other items in the environment, such as a ramp or rings. These colorful Hacky Sacks can be dropped, rolled, tossed, kicked, and more, and children will challenge themselves to use the balls to create complex games.

These inviting wood stones are smooth to the touch. To develop imaginative play and increase complexity, you can offer concrete figures of people of many backgrounds and abilities in a basket for children to use as they desire. Seeing children and adults who look like them and their family increases children's motivation; noticing those who look different engages their mind to learn about diverse people.

The Importance of Critical Thinking

Developing critical thinking is crucial for children with diverse abilities so they can make effective decisions and increase their independence. Integrate complexity, novelty, and wonder into the environment to ensure that children develop higher-order critical-thinking skills. The path to developing critical thinking for children with diverse abilities starts with expressing their feelings. Once they begin to recognize their emotions, adults can help them make sense of their thoughts and make logical connections to their ideas so that they can move sequentially from one idea to the next. To help children develop truly abstract-thinking skills, we need to ask questions related to their feelings. Instead of asking a broad, open-ended question such as, "What did you do this morning?" ask inquiry questions that connect to what they did, what they felt, or what they experienced: "What did you discover when you played with the wooden stones this morning?" or "I noticed you screamed when the wooden stones kept falling. Can you tell me what you were feeling?"

Children are constantly processing information, discerning visual, auditory, and sensory messages from the environment. The brain helps children organize, analyze, compare, contrast, make meaning, and define everything they hear, see, and feel. Loose Parts play lets children with diverse abilities experience their senses and make meaning of their perceptions, ideas, and interests. Understanding how children think helps educators provide play opportunities that deepen their critical thinking.

True learning is not acquiring, memorizing, and repeating facts. My grandparents had a parrot that was taught to repeat a few words (some I would rather not utter). The parrot was incredibly skillful at repetition, especially when given a treat after each word. Just because the parrot repeated these words did not mean it knew what they meant. I am not comparing children to my grandparents' parrot, but the analogy helps us see why we must go beyond repetition. Memorization and repetition seldom help children use the information to build more complex and accurate understandings. Thus they may misinterpret and misuse the information. Because facts that we repeat and memorize are often ephemeral and disappear from our minds soon after taking a test, we want to ensure that children make sense of information in a way that deepens their ability to learn. More important, we want to make sure the information connects to something meaningful to them so they can fully process and understand it.

In this current educational climate where there is so much pressure on educators to teach children specific content knowledge, it is even more imperative to focus on the deeper meaning of thinking as the root of real learning. Learning happens when children are encouraged to think as they play and explore open-ended tools and materials such as Loose Parts. When there is something important and worthwhile to think about and a reason to think deeply, children experience the kind of learning that has a powerful influence not only in the short term but for the long haul. They not only learn; they learn how to learn (Ritchhart, Church, and Morrison 2011). Learning how to learn is particularly important for children with cognitive differences who need concrete experiences and emotional connections to make sense of their world.

Educators can help children dissect their ideas and thinking by breaking their thought process into small concepts. Children need to be able to respond to *what, where, when, who, why*, and *how* questions and compare and contrast ideas and group them into categories. Comparing, contrasting, and categorizing is critical to finding patterns and meaning in the world. Loose Parts offer multiple affordances to categorize in ways that are meaningful to children with diverse abilities. Simple changes such as educators separating crayons and markers by color help children notice differences and facilitate access while promoting an understanding of color.

Observing children helps educators design ecosystems with a culture where thinking is valued, visible, and integrated into every aspect of the day. Thinking is not only learned; instead, it is a disposition and habit of mind that is enculturated into everyday experiences and interactions (Ritchhart, Turner, and Hadar 2009). The authors discuss the importance of creating an ecosystem founded in eight pillars of practice: (1) the physical environment of the classroom, (2) the use of language, (3) children and educator interactions, (4) the allocation of time, (5) the creation of learning opportunities, (6) the use of structures and routines to scaffold and support thinking and learning, (7) the modeling of thinking, and (8) the setting of expectations for thinking. One way to accomplish the eight pillars of practice is through thinking routines, which are simple patterns of thinking that can be used over and over (see examples). Thinking routines are made visible through documentation, narratives, and thinking maps (webs). Educators share the thinking routines with children, colleagues, and families. Thinking routines provide groups with a visible representation of how their ideas, theories, questions, and reflections develop. Thinking routines also help develop a structure that guides children as they play and learn.

Curate Loose Parts that can be sorted, classified, analyzed, and integrated into construction and symbolic play—this supports children's critical thinking in how they use Loose Parts to express their ideas. For instance, Lydale has an interest in connecting and disconnecting. She often goes directly to the area where the pop-up tubes (plastic corrugated tubes) are kept. She also lines up chairs and ties ribbons to connect them. She moves fast from one idea to the next. The educators notice her interest and bring other Loose Parts to connect and disconnect: nuts and bolts, large paper clips, silicone beads to string and pull, and pop tubes that can be connected. The educator shares with Lydale her observations about the thinking that is taking place as Lydale explores the connecting schema.

Language is essential in a culture that promotes critical thinking. When educators create opportunities to engage in conversation and create thinking routines, they support children with diverse abilities and children learning a second language to express their ideas, feelings, and understandings. The thinking-routines process sends the message to children that they are competent and capable, and that the educator values their participation and contributions to the classroom ecosystem. Include the six *W* questions (what, where, when, who, why, and how) in all conversations and explorations to strengthen children's critical-thinking skills. An educator may say to a child, "I wonder what will happen when you put the box on top of the tower." "What do you notice about the base that supports the tower?" or "Think about where you can place the last box so that the tower does not topple over." By asking questions closely related to what the child is doing, the educator promotes hypothesis generation and problem solving.

Thinking routines require the gift of time. Planning flexible schedules that allow children to develop and test hypotheses, make mistakes, and analyze outcomes helps them develop critical-thinking skills. Ian, a four-year-old with neurodiversity, recently discovered the colorful wooden Loose Parts on the shelves. He enjoys arranging them in different configurations, sorting and classifying them by size and color. Sean, the educator, notices how Ian classifies the items and wants to expand his thinking. He approaches Ian and engages him in a compare and contrast thinking routine, saying, "I see that you classified the Loose Parts by color, shape, and size. How many different ways can you find to group them?" Ian stops and observes the Loose Parts' characteristics and quietly replies, "By how they feel." Sean responds, "Yes, by the texture. What other ways to classify can you think of?" The conversation continues as Ian arranges the colorful wooden Loose Parts into a circle. Sean notices the design and says, "Ian, you created a mandala. Remember, we looked at mandalas on Monday?" Ian smiles and continues to design using the Loose Parts.

One of educators' most important roles is creating play opportunities that challenge children to solve problems. Playing with Loose Parts engages children in developing problem-solving skills, though children with diverse abilities may need extra support in this. For instance, Amelie is building with the mini tree stump blocks. The irregular shapes and uneven surfaces of the blocks create a challenge for Amelie. Solange, the educator, approaches Amelie and asks, "I wonder what would happen if you use the tree stump blocks with the unit blocks? How will the differences help you balance the blocks to create the structure you planned?" Solange uses an analogy thinking routine to encourage comparing two different items. By asking questions, Solange is guiding Amelie to problem solve and change her strategies.

Thinking processes are built into our brains; we use them automatically all the time. But we don't always use them efficiently. Efficient learners know how to access different modes of thinking consciously and apply them to different kinds of tasks. This process involves metacognition, or thinking about thinking. Metacognitive strategies help students analyze the task or problem, recognize what kind of thinking is required, and activate the right cognitive processes for the task at hand. A student with strong metacognitive skills understands the different modes of thinking and can apply them deliberately and effectively.

When educators take time to look at thinking from different perspectives, we become alert to children's metacognition. Teachers help students build metacognitive

The following are thinking routines and questions that promote critical thinking:

- Hypothesis: If I do [this action: _____], [this result: _____] may happen.
- Reason and logic: Present a passage from a book or a small provocation for children to think about. Engage children in inquiry by asking a question such as "What makes Ada a scientist?" Children can argue their ideas and present different choices. These are some of my favorite books for starting conversations:
  - *Ada Twist, Scientist* by Andrea Beaty
  - *Be a Maker* by Katey Howes
  - *Beyond the Pond* by Joseph Kuefler
- **Cause and effect:** Do towers always fall when the base is smaller? Are there times when the base can be smaller but the tower won't fall? How else can we investigate this issue?
- **Analogy:** I wonder what would happen if you used two different sets of blocks. How are the blocks different? How will the differences help make a stabler base?
- **Classification:** How many ways can you find to group the bottle caps? Can they be classified by color, shape, or size?
- **Evidence:** How do you know that the blocks worked? How did you know that . . . ?
- **Possibility:** What else can you use? How else can you combine the [Loose Parts]? What other possible combinations can you generate?
- **Imagination/Creativity:** What could be invented to do [this action]? What do you think can happen here? What is your idea? I wonder . . .
- **Perspective:** How would other children respond to your idea? How will this affect other people? What do you think other people will think? How can you include other children to work on your idea?
- **Define:** List the facts, details, and key information you know about a topic or term. For example, "Whales are mammals, there are many types, and some species are bigger than others. They live in different parts of the world's oceans."

skills by providing explicit instruction and modeling for each of the eight core metacognitive skills (cause and effect, analogy, classification, evidence, possibility, creativity, perspective, define). Doing so lets students get a glimpse "under the hood" of their own thinking so that they understand how their brains work and what they need to do to activate these processes. Critical thinking takes a lot of patience and perseverance, but it is one of the most valuable life skills you can foster.

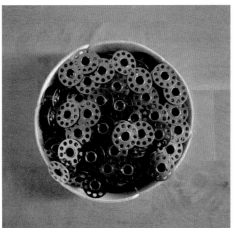

Loose Parts such as sewing bobbins tap into children's creativity and cognitive flexibility as they seek other materials to combine with the spools, then pair them with wooden arcs to test attributes such as speed and velocity.

The multifaceted surfaces and varied sizes and shapes of these wooden stones engage intentional thinking as children plan how they will construct and design with them. For children who are beginning to develop frustration tolerance or who are working on planning, use fewer stones and set out the largest stones with wide surface areas to increase their success.

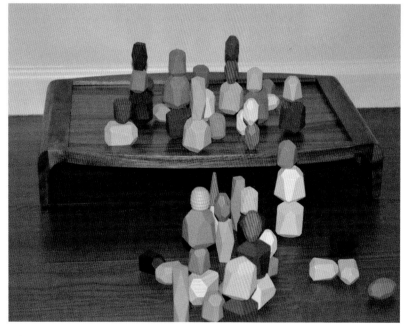

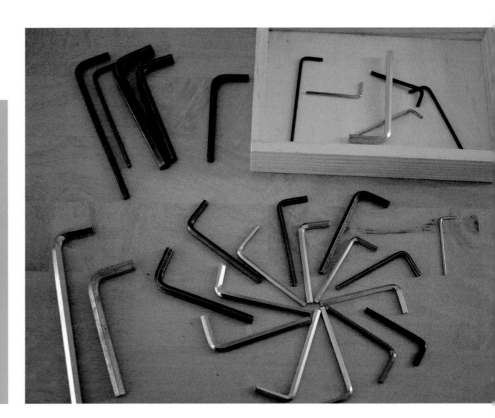

Real metal hex wrenches lend themselves well to critical thinking as children seriate, design, and sort them by size, weight, and color. As children are cognitively and physically ready, incorporate real-life hex screws and a wooden pegboard with drill holes for children to practice using the tools.

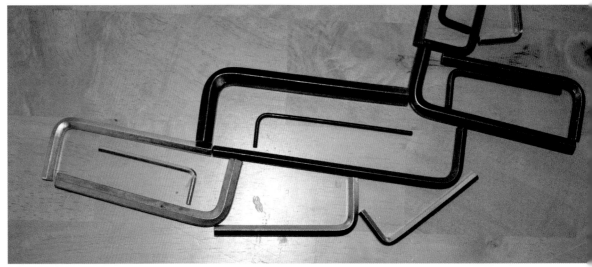

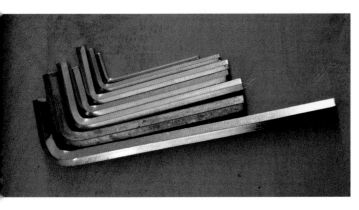

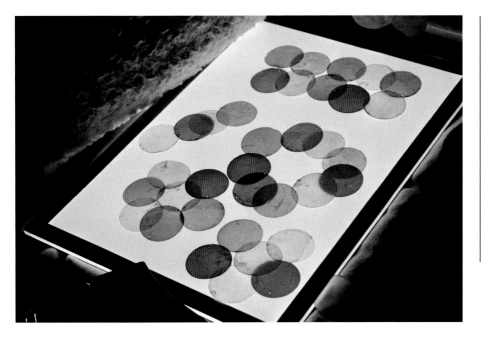

Children use a light table to test how light travels through different-colored shells, glitter wands, and more. Cushions and pillows make spaces comfortable and inviting.

Truly open-ended play allows children to synthesize their own meaning for the materials and critically analyze and change components to meet their needs. The natural blocks and sand could be a farm, then become a forest, a beach, or any other imaginable scene.

Wonder and Curiosity

Curiosity is the gift and pleasure of knowing or learning something new. Wonder is that ongoing sense of surprise that keeps us researching, exploring, and learning. Children's sense of wonder and intense curiosity leads them to pursue answers relentlessly. Children want to know, to see, and to experience new things. Curiosity can be defined as the recognition, pursuit, and intense desire to explore novel, challenging, and unknown adventures. The brain's chemistry changes when we become curious, helping us understand and retain information. Curiosity prepares the brain for learning, so it becomes a fast-moving information-gathering machine that encourages further wonderment and learning. Curiosity is a fundamental impulse in humans, and education needs to be based on this behavior. Cultivating childhood wonder and joy requires educators to do less of what doesn't matter and more of what does. Constantly pushing children with diverse abilities to do more or encounter overly daunting challenges can lead them to lose their sense of wonder.

Loose Parts provide novelty, multiple affordances, and ways to explore, putting children in charge of satisfying their curiosity while eliciting wonder. Curiosity motivates children to act and think in new ways, investigate, be immersed, and learn about their immediate target's qualities. It is a vital, motivating aspect of learning and knowledge gathering. For example, Raúl, who is four years old and experiences some neurodiversity challenges, is incredibly curious about water's qualities. He spends time playing at the water table and enjoys pouring water from one container to another. His curiosity sparks him to ask questions: "What makes water? What floats and what sinks in the water? What happens to water when it is cold or hot?" This intense curiosity leads Annette, the educator, to bring Raúl ice cubes. On the first day, she makes the ice cubes with just water and later adds liquid watercolor. She gives Raúl time to explore the ice cubes, which hold his curiosity for a while. As Raúl continues to ask questions, Annette adds flashlights to explore the ice cubes' transparency and color. She makes more ice cubes, this time freezing colorful silicone beads inside the cubes. Raul watches as the sun melts the cubes and asks many questions: "How long will it take? What happens to the beads? Will they also melt?" Annette invites other children to join, and together they write their questions and responses. Raúl feels welcomed and enjoys the conversations with other children.

Curious children are in constant search of novelty. They create learning opportunities by asking questions and exploring Loose Parts in new and inventive ways. They are interested in facts, ideas, and opinions. As they pursue their curiosity, they are prepared to find novel ideas and new perspectives. One question leads to the next, and off they go into the path of learning. This process requires flexibility, self-regulation, and adaptation. Children respond to the environment by making rapid cognitive judgments. They first decide whether an object or tool offers something novel, complex, or challenging. They then consider whether they can manage the object or tool successfully. The differences in how children appraise Loose Parts correspond to individual differences in curiosity and wonder (Silvia 2006).

To create wonder and curiosity, we must start by creating a safe and familiar place where children can explore, test ideas, and ask questions without feeling judged or criticized. As adults, we know that when we feel confident and safe, we are more willing to attempt something new. When we are overwhelmed, we look for familiarity and comfort. The same is true for children with diverse abilities. The challenge for early childhood educators is designing a classroom ecosystem that is safe and familiar but also stimulating. Encouraging curiosity and a sense of wonder is a significant challenge when the classroom has children with varying temperaments and different ways of exploring and making sense of the world. Yet promoting curiosity in children, especially for children with diverse abilities, may be a meaningful, underrecognized way to address the achievement gap. After all, curiosity is a life force. It is vital to happiness, intellectual growth, and overall well-being. Giving free rein to children's curiosity helps them develop much-needed social skills, resilience, self-awareness, integrity, resourcefulness, creativity, empathy, compassion, and knowingness. Curiosity is a foundation for early learning and beyond. This is especially true for children with diverse abilities, who may need extra support to feel confident about their capacities and achievements. The educator's role is to regulate, guide, and nurture children's curiosity by designing an ecosystem in which provocations and invitations captivate their curiosity. These catalysts help children stay focused and delve deeper into their sense of wonder.

Don't give in to the temptation to reward children when their curiosity meets a required outcome. Instead, support children when they actively engage their curiosity. Describe the questions they ask and how their investigation is deepening their learning. Appreciate their willingness to try something new or discover a novel solution. Let children know that they are valued for their curiosity and sense of wonder by responding to and supporting their ideas and interests. Promoting curiosity requires educators to let go of curricular expectations and instead learn to explain to peers and adults how curiosity leads children to engage in intellectual learning.

Start with engaging your own curiosity and sense of wonder. Be playful and enjoy the power of creativity. We live in a culture that mostly values things that have a purpose, application, or benefit. We focus on productivity, financial health, and specific accomplishments. We fill our days with to-do lists. We forget that children's nature is more qualitative, and they are not concerned with completing a task or meeting a productivity outcome.

Approach the way you design the physical classroom ecosystem, explorations, and activities by embracing change and uncertainty, which are necessary characteristics of curiosity. When educators become researchers with children, they are open to the multiple possibilities that children's curiosity offers. They follow the children's lead and let go of specific expectations. Children with diverse abilities need to see adults model how to handle uncertainty and tolerate change. Children need to know that educators have a noncritical and playful attitude. Show understanding and patience as children with diverse abilities approach Loose Parts in a variety of ways. Give them the time to follow their curiosity, and be prepared to guide them as you notice they need support. Look for the moment when you see a new spark, and ask a question that invites children to see a problem as a mystery that needs to be solved. Observing and responding during these learning moments is crucial to keeping children's curiosity and sense of wonder going.

Curiosity is contagious among children, so help it spread by creating opportunities for collaborative play. Place Loose Parts in areas that allow a group of children to work together. Listen to their conversations and stay close to give the children with diverse abilities support as needed. When children play together, they cross-pollinate ideas and interests. They challenge and support one another's curiosity. Observe and notice children's responses and attitudes toward group interactions. Be prepared to serve as a supporter to ensure that children with diverse abilities are included in the play.

Simple invitations such as this color poster develop attention skills and build visual discrimination. Inspired by the poster, children can explore the three-dimensional acrylic Loose Parts. They can compare the colors and consider how a two-dimensional shape can also be replicated as a three-dimensional shape.

Photos: Diane Spahn, Director of Education, Kodo Kids

Cork blocks of a variety of shapes and sizes support wonderment as children explore weight, balance, and space. The cork blocks can offer complexity and provide a safe source of play for children adapting to auditory stimulation, as the blocks fall quietly.

Photo: Kasey Kile, Director of Professional Development, Kodo Kids

The more affordances a Loose Part has, the more opportunities for wonder and experimentation. Children practice attention, planning, organization, prioritization, and self-monitoring skills when they turn simple, colorful tubes into designs, chutes, tracks, hoops, games, and more!

Swirls of frozen color captivate children, sparking their curiosity about the ice cubes' changing appearance as they melt. Support children with tactile or temperature sensitivities by providing towels to dry their hands during play.

Depending on their sensory needs, some children benefit from suspended swinging while manipulating items like ribbons. This supports their vestibular sense while also providing a sense of wonder. Start with slow swaying, observe, and adjust their input appropriately. Consider consulting a pediatric occupational therapist as well.

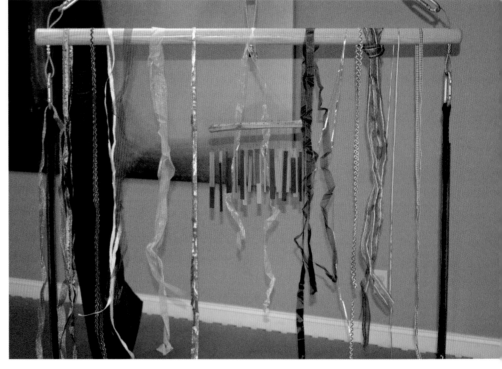

Chapter 5
Engaging Identity, Agency, and Relationships

The meanings attributed to extraordinary bodies reside not in inherent physical flaws, but in social relationships in which one group is legitimized by possessing valued physical characteristics and maintains its ascendancy and its self-identity by systematically imposing the role of cultural or corporeal inferiority. —Rosemarie Garland-Thomson

As human beings, we become more aware of who we are through strong relationships. Young children experience their world as an ecosystem in which they are an individual and at the same time have interconnected relationships. Through the relationships that children build, they discover their identity and learn to understand different perspectives. Their relationships affect virtually all aspects of their development—cognitive, social, emotional, physical, creative, and moral. Relationship building describes the process of establishing emotional connections that are based on trust and intimacy. It starts with bonding and attachment with primary caregivers and expands to other adults in children's lives. The renowned educator and TV personality Fred Rogers thoughtfully and consistently planned the language he used in his PBS television show to intentionally help children understand the power of relationships. Mr. Rogers often advised children to listen to their favorite grown-ups for instruction on where to play safely. He reminded us that in times of crisis, we look for helpers. When we hear his advice, we must recognize that we are the adults he refers to. We have the power to listen, honor, and respect children. We must build trust so children learn to establish relationships throughout their lives. This is crucial for children with diverse abilities. They need to trust themselves and trust their environment. They must feel competent and be seen as active and respected members of a community. Developing communal attachment is a key component to developing identity.

As educators, we must create ecosystems that support children's identity, agency, and relationships. These ecosystems must build nurturing relationships with adults and encourage interactions with peers. Children, including children with diverse abilities, learn how to be friends, engage in reciprocal interactions, and take the desires of others into account as they interact with peers. But just being around other children is not enough. Developing true friendships is essential, as children learn and play more competently in the rapport created with friends than when facing the social challenges of interacting with casual acquaintances or unfamiliar peers. Loose Parts can facilitate the building of relationships as adults present provocations that engage children in collaborative play.

For example, Simone and Anna spend time together both at preschool and at home. Their families are good friends and get together regularly. Simone is quiet and often takes time processing information. However, that changes when Anna arrives at the preschool. Simone runs up to Anna and hugs her. They look around together and notice what is new. They sit next to a set of cork blocks and cardboard pieces. They begin to build, and in silence they point to different things and nod when they agree to continue their building. Even though Simone's ability to orally communicate is limited, she and Anna have discovered a powerful form of communication. Their relationship is helping them both grow in empathy and care. Often other children join in the play and are slowly learning to understand Simone's gestures. They are building their identity, acquiring a strong sense of agency, and connecting with each other.

Identity

Identity connects to the way children express themselves both as individuals and as members of groups. Identity defines us because it contains our personality traits, our abilities, and the social roles we play. In this regard, having a diverse ability is an identity context that establishes membership in a group that is often subjected to marginalization, prejudice, and discrimination.

Language and perceptions matter. The way we perceive children with diverse abilities and how we refer to them has a profound effect on their identity. Many children with diverse abilities ultimately find opportunity, hope, compassion, and gratitude in their defined identity. They build a cohesive vision that incorporates their abilities, strengths, and capacities. Children who feel worthy and capable are more optimistic and engage other children in play. A healthy sense of identity helps children be more open to other communities, not fear differences, and even feel better about themselves.

Both implicit and explicit messages affect the identity of children with diverse abilities and how they perceive themselves as active community members. Children are children first, but while their label does not define them, it is part of their identity. The disability should not be seen as a limitation or something "bad." Instead, we want to ensure that our perspective supports children in discovering their strengths. Too often children with diverse abilities are seen from a deficit-based perspective. Ableism, or the discrimination of and social prejudice against people with disabilities based on the belief that typical abilities are superior, takes over. The responsibilities of experts, including educators, are often seen as identifying, advising, recommending a diagnosis, and providing treatment. When educators concentrate on "fixing" children with diverse abilities, they focus on the label rather than each child's capacities. Creating such an image of a child can have a significant negative impact on their identity. Shifting these beliefs requires educators to reflect on their perceptions and expectations of children. This is the first step in creating an inclusive environment that supports the healthy identity of children with diverse abilities.

Because of its implications for how we may be perceived as early childhood educators, I share the following story hesitantly. However, I still find the story worth sharing to encourage us to reflect on our power over children. I preface the story by saying that this is the exception and I hope not the reality for many children.

Once when I was observing children, I noticed an educator's hard tone as she talked to Mario, who was new to the program. His family was originally from Mexico. Mario would hug the children as he walked into the program. The educator would always step in and say, "Don't touch other children," "Stop. You can't do that," "Use your words," and "I don't understand what you are saying." Often these harsh words were accompanied by physical actions that restrained the child. I realized the educator thought this child was autistic and did not have boundaries. She perceived Mario as dangerous and needing fixing and saw herself as protecting the rest of the children. As the days progressed, the situation escalated. Mario's family was informed by the educator and administrator that they would be referred for special services. They suspected Mario of being autistic because "he speaks in gibberish," and "his lack of boundaries may hurt other children." This entire interaction stuck with me for a while. I was concerned about Mario's well-being. On a day when I was again observing, Mario approached me. In a clear voice, he told me, "Mi abuelita y abuelito van a venir a visitarme" ("My grandma and grandpa are coming to visit me"). Mario then gave me a hug and pulled my hand and invited me to sit on the floor. He used blocks and other Loose Parts to build an airplane. He proceeded to tell me in Spanish, "This is the plane, and here is where they are sitting." He was articulate, and his thought process was clear and organized. In this scenario, the "expert" assumptions created a situation that could have further affected Mario's identity. He did not speak "gibberish"; he was imitating English-language phonemes, which is a typical process children use when they are making sense of a new language. He did not demonstrate the signs of neurodiversity and did know boundaries. People greet one another with a kiss and a hug in Mario's family and culture. To him, physical greetings were a sign of respect and how people entered relationships.

As educators, we have tremendous power, and what we say and do affects the children in our care. Our responsibility is to continually question our assumptions and reflect on our perceptions. We also must recognize that we are not trained nor in a position to assess disabilities.

As we consider the identity formation of children with diverse abilities, we must also consider the identity of their families. Raising a family is a challenge under the best of circumstances. When families learn that one of their children diverges from typical development, whether medical, cognitive, neurological, sensory, or physical, their stress increases as they confront a compounding set of challenges. Educators can support them in finding their identity as a family with diverse abilities. The best place to start is focusing on the child's strengths. Families should not have to deal with a list of what their children can't do. Instead, they need to see that there are many strengths and that there is hope. When families make sense of their child's diverse abilities and focus on the strengths of the child and the whole family, they can create a positive identity that helps them advocate for their child and access resources—financial, emotional, and other support services.

One way educators can connect with the family's identity and purpose is by recognizing their culture. For example, respect for nature is integral to many Indigenous communities of North America. Involving all family members in traditions that communicate respect for nature, such as telling stories, using natural Loose Parts, or creating collaborative art, can strengthen the family's identity and help them thrive in a supportive environment.

Fortunately, we have one of the best vehicles to support children's identity: play. Psychoanalyst Erik Erikson (1977) saw play as the process children use to find their identity and master the skills needed for everyday life. Erikson explained, "The growing child's play (and that is what a long childhood is for) is the training ground for the experience of a leeway of imaginative choices within an existence governed and guided by roles and visions"(78). Educators can make intentional decisions in choosing Loose Parts to support identity formation. When children play with Loose Parts, they are in charge. They make decisions, design, engineer, and develop their creativity. Loose Parts with mirrors let children see themselves represented. Loose Parts that let children express their stories help them make meaning of their current situation. Loose Parts that provide comfort, such as soft blankets and felted animals, support children's capacities and promote a sense of well-being. Loose Parts used in a group exploration promote a sense of belonging. They give children control of their actions, furthering their sense of agency.

Art in the Forest

Nothing is more powerful than working together to accomplish a mutual goal. For example, Isabella and Mateo visited the local sequoia forest. With permission from the park rangers, they collected pine needles and pine cone scale seeds. They brought their treasures into the classroom to share with the other children. Mateo, Isabella, and Alfonzo spent the day working on a collective mural, and other children joined in throughout the day. Alfonzo, who has Down syndrome, was enthralled with the different seeds and watched closely as the children combined them into intricate flower designs. Suddenly, Alfonzo left the area and came back with leaves, which he added to the flowers. He smiled and pointed to his contribution. Isabella said, "Trae más hojas" ("Bring more leaves") in a wonderful moment of inclusion and collaboration.

Cutouts from recycled boxes are one example of Loose Parts that enable self-expression and agency. Children develop their identity as they create limitless designs that are meaningful to them. The various sizes support children with diverse abilities.

Simple materials such as metal feather bookmarks spur children to ask one another questions and collaboratively decide together how best to use the Loose Parts or combine them with other materials. These interactions create a sense of inclusion for children with diverse abilities.

Place napkin rings alongside other metal Loose Parts on a child-accessible shelf. Allowing children to decide whether they will use them alone or combine them with other materials supports their self-efficacy and resiliency. Being an active agent in play and effecting change in their environment are both key in a child's development of agency.

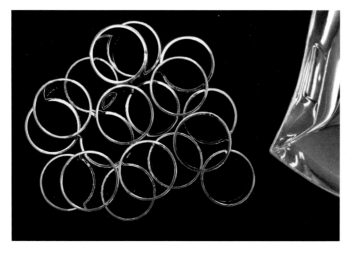

Developing a Sense of Agency

As children make choices and decisions, they develop a sense of agency, or the motivation to achieve a goal. Agency allows children to generate, monitor, and plan their own learning and manage their cognitive, affective, and behavioral processes. A sense of agency helps children move from feeling as though things simply happen to them to taking control of their actions. Children with diverse abilities continuously navigate medical, social, emotional, and cognitive stressors. Developing a sense of agency gives them a feeling of belonging and power over their lives. They need to see their power in initiating play and learning and to recognize that they can affect the community and the world. When children with diverse abilities feel that they belong and are trusted as valued members of a community, they thrive and develop a strong energy. Creating ecosystems in which children control their play is essential to fully engage them in developing agency. Once again, Loose Parts give children the control in deciding how and when they will use them, as the following story illustrates.

Martina has been enthralled by the stones in the outdoor ecosystem. She often lines up the rocks, and lately she has started stacking them. Martina starts with two rocks at a time and eventually stacks a third rock. When she starts adding a fourth rock, they topple over. The educators hear Martina scream in what appears to be a moment of frustration. They step back and watch. Martina stops screaming and carefully observes each rock. She touches them on all sides, brings them close to her eyes, and then places the flatter rocks at the bottom. The selection process continues, and Martina manages to build a twelve-stone tower. She stands up, looks at the educators, and smiles. Her sense of agency is palpable. She has learned to trust the ecosystem, the adults, and, most important, herself. Martina wants to accomplish something important to her, and she seems to be aware of the points of frustration and has learned to manage them. Martina also demonstrates trust in her own capacities and knows that some tasks may be difficult, but she can conquer them with consistency and patience.

The beauty of Loose Parts is how they challenge children to think differently, see themselves as capable and competent, and learn with resilience and confidence. As educators, we must suspend our expectations of what children must do with the Loose Parts and instead reflect on how our expectations interfere with children's play. For children to develop a strong sense of self, they must gain power over their play. Children are frequently confronted with a world of ready-made materials that center on adults' perspectives. They are given premade toys, and adults give them ideas for what to do with them. It is not surprising that in the last two decades, children's interest and capacity to play are disappearing. Instead, children seem preoccupied with the end product, making something that fulfills adult expectations. In his book *Toys and Reasons: Stages in the Ritualization of Experience*, Erik Erikson (1977) argues that when children are confronted with a premanufactured, ready-made toy "world" (houses, trees, fences, people, vehicles, animals, and so forth), they seem to be most eager to show that they know how to arrange them in a functional way. More like a test, then, their performance reflects primarily their mental capacity (or incapacity) to organize a classified universe. Rather, when adults provide Loose Parts play opportunities, children take leadership over their play. Loose Parts invite children to structure the available space with innovative ideas and give them the space to imagine freely.

Rather than telling children how to use Loose Parts, educators must step back and trust that children know what to do. Let's pledge to restore play and let children lead us on the journey. The more we trust children, the more they will learn to trust us, which will carry over as they build daily interactions with others. They come to understand that just like they themselves have the agency to create, other children have the same capacities.

You are probably wondering what your role is as an educator in supporting children with diverse abilities to develop agency and control over their lives. You may also ask, "How can Loose Parts support the process?" The answer is multi-faceted; however, we can start by redefining our image of children. The beginning of this chapter mentions how words matter. The same is true in how we think of children. In the schools of Reggio Emilia in Italy, children are valued as capable, competent, creative, innovative thinkers, risk-takers, and many more positive attributes. The adults trust the children but also trust themselves because they take the time to question their assumptions and practices. They observe what children are doing, and they see themselves as researchers along with the children. Educators are open to learning and being vulnerable. They don't need to know everything, and they find joy in their unexpected discoveries from the journey. As adults, we must find the courage to see children differently than what we expect them to be.

A Sense of Efficacy and Mastery

As adults, when we make informed choices, we feel more in control of our decisions and better follow through with our goals. The same is true for children, including children with diverse abilities. In making choices, children begin to develop self-efficacy, or the belief that they can perform a task or control a situation. Influential social cognitive psychologist Albert Bandura (1997) describes how self-efficacy is a person's belief in their ability to succeed in a particular situation. Bandura argues that these beliefs determine how people think, behave, and feel. Children with diverse abilities need to develop the belief that they can accomplish their goals and succeed.

Agency and efficacy go hand in hand, but they serve a different purpose in the achievement of goals. Agency is the ability to make choices and act upon those choices to change your life. In other words, it is the power to take action. Self-efficacy gives children the ability to reflect on their thinking, their choices, and their beliefs about their capacity to make changes in their lives. In other words, self-efficacy helps children develop intentionality and purpose. It allows them to judge how their actions affect what they do and make corrections. Self-efficacy provides self-awareness and awareness of how our actions affect other people's lives. Both agency and efficacy are essential to function and succeed in society.

For young children, making choices and developing self-efficacy must happen in a holistic and developmentally appropriate way as you respond to their interests and ideas. Loose Parts serve as a vehicle to support children's choices because they are in full control of the objects. When children with diverse abilities play with Loose Parts, they are making their own decisions. They learn to make mistakes, and they eventually develop a can-do attitude. They see themselves as capable and competent despite the challenges presented by their diverse abilities. A sense of agency and self-efficacy increases children's ability to think productively by applying positive-thinking skills when facing a challenge. It also helps them develop motivation and effort to accomplish a goal or task.

A child with high self-efficacy believes they have the skills to help them steer through life and reach their goals. A sense of mastery comes when a child truly feels they can accomplish what they set out to do. It helps them acquire expertise. It happens when a child equates success to something they can control. For example, they may think, "I can stack all the tree cookies to build a tall tower all on my own." Mastery reinforces stronger self-efficacy beliefs. In contrast, a child does not develop a sense of mastery when they equate success to something out of their control. They blame success and failure on external factors. For example, a child may think, "I was not able to stack the tree cookies because Ronald kept knocking them down," or "I did not stack the tree cookies because the teacher did not give me enough time."

Perhaps most important, self-efficacy is about learning how to persevere when you fail. It is about becoming the master of your own capacities and abilities. For example, Luis sits at a table using tongs to transfer small felt balls into a container. This is his first time using the tongs, which he holds with his one functioning hand. He attentively picks up a ball and carefully moves his hand to the top of the container, where he releases hold of the tongs and watches as the felt ball falls into the container. More than one ball rolls off the table when it misses the target, but Luis stays focused and keeps going. He displays a strong sense of agency, and his efficacy grows with each ball dropped into the container. The educators watch and give Luis the space to keep on working on this new skill. After about twenty minutes, the container is filled. Luis smiles, gets up, and walks around the table to pick up the felt balls that rolled away. Luis is satisfied with his accomplishment, and he does not need to be praised or rewarded. He knows what he is capable of, and he continues to grow in his ability to use his body to accomplish his goals.

Imagine children who are hospitalized and have limited opportunities to make choices. Allowing them to make choices in their play helps them develop agency and self-efficacy to manage the ongoing interventions they must endure. Educators can embrace the challenge of creating Loose Parts opportunities that can be used in small spaces and meet hygienic requirements. Invite families to create a box with easy-to-clean Loose Parts that can be kept in the hospital to involve the whole family in the process of play. An easily cleaned acrylic tray can engage children when they have to stay in bed. Children can squirt water with droppers and use plastic tubing to become familiar with a medical tool, thus normalizing the hospital experience and making medical equipment and procedures feel less foreign.

As I have visited different programs and observed children's interactions with peers, adults, and the environment, I have noticed that the image of children and adults there influences children's sense of autonomy and their behaviors. Having the autonomy to make choices and guide their learning based on interests helps children engage their sense of competency and recognize their strengths and abilities. An ecosystem designed to build autonomy in children goes a long way in supporting each child's holistic development. Inviting children to participate in making the rules of where the Loose Parts can go in the environment and how they will be picked up and reorganized helps children manage their environment and builds trust with the educators. Most important, educators can meet children's needs to have some choice and control, instilling in them the ownership that allows them to take responsibility for their own learning. When educators share power with children, not only is their work easier, but it also helps children develop a sense of responsibility and motivation that transcends everything except their desire to learn.

Building Resilience and Protective Factors

Agency and self-efficacy promote greater resiliency—the ability to adapt when there is a crisis, trauma, tragedy, threat, or significant stressor and bounce back to a feeling of normalcy afterward. We know that life does not have a map that is easy to follow. Just like the trials of 2020 and 2021, life is filled with unexpected challenges. We all experience twists and turns, like fear, the death of a loved one, a life-altering accident, a severe illness, or a diverse ability. Each change in circumstance affects people differently, bringing a unique flood of thoughts, strong emotions, and uncertainty. Yet people generally adapt well over time to life-changing or stressful situations, in part thanks to resilience. While many of these moments are painful, they don't have to determine our lives. When children play, they find hope and strength in their own abilities. The power of Loose Parts play helps them bounce back because they gain control over their abilities. When children play, they become more resilient and are better able to overcome difficult circumstances.

As children play with Loose Parts, they make sense of what they are experiencing. Storytelling with Loose Parts puts children in charge of the ever-evolving situations they face. Loose Parts help children create imaginary worlds where they can change the ending to their own stories. It helps them understand that resilience is ever-evolving and that nothing stays the same forever, even if it feels as if nothing is changing. Through play, children explore new possibilities, adapt to old situations, and control their circumstances. They learn that their disability does not define them. It is just another part of their identity. The adults must focus on encouraging children's efforts to make choices and decisions instead of praising their abilities. Children with diverse abilities, in particular, need to know that effort will lead them to meet their own expectations, and they do not always have to please the adults in their lives. For instance, Rogelio, who has low muscle strength, has a strong desire to join other children as they play outdoors. He watches from his adaptive chair and claps as he sees the children playing in the swing they created with rope and pieces of wood. Jonathan notices Rogelio clapping, and he stops swinging and asks the educators if they can make a swing so Rogelio can participate. The educators invite Arturo, Rogelio's dad, to help the children make an adaptive swing. Together they plan, create drawings, and gather materials. They determine that a car tire with a built-in wooden base will give Rogelio the support he needs. Arturo builds the tire swing and brings it to the program. With the help of the children, they hang the swing from a strong branch. Rogelio uses his walker to get to the swing. The children clap as Rogelio climbs into the swing with the help of his father. Classmates gather around and encourage Rogelio to move his feet and make the swing go faster. This joyful story of empathy, care, collaboration, and community building is a testament to agency and resiliency.

To build resilience in children's lives, educators must boost the processes that protect development from negative impacts, including social interactions and relationships, ecosystems of support, adaptation to the environment, and the child's sense of trust, autonomy, and initiative. These processes or protective factors can make a difference in the developmental outcomes of children with diverse abilities. When educators intentionally design ecosystems that give children autonomy to take charge of their choices and learning, they are

strengthening protective factors that will further support children's development. Studies on resilience and protective factors conclude that resilience usually arises from ordinary adaptive processes, rather than rare or extraordinary ones. This finding allows educators to focus on creating ecosystems that build on the strengths of children with diverse abilities while accommodating their different abilities (Luthar 2003).

Children can explore transparency and color mixing with translucent colored cups. For items set on the ground or within an enclosure, ensure that all children can physically access the materials. An occupational therapist or other specialist may recommend adaptive seating or trunk-support cushions for optimal positioning during floor play.

Providing acrylic trays and movable containers without directions for an activity builds autonomous thought. For children who are working on attention skills or developing agency, placing color cards in the trays to sort and match the felt balls adds structure to the task. This is also a safe exploration when children must stay in bed due to illness.

Metal canisters and bottle caps support children's agency as they use the Loose Parts to make popping sounds and rhythms, count, stack, open and close, insert, compare size, and more. For children sensitive to sound, present fewer items and place them in a noise-reducing container on a carpeted area.

Drawing their own design on puzzle pieces builds executive functioning skills such as planning and decision-making, and gives children control over the puzzle's outcome. To accommodate various ages and skill levels, provide larger puzzle pieces or fewer total pieces.

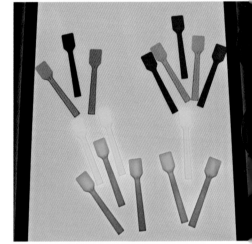

Promote agency for children who can see only shadows or children developing visual-spatial and visual-perceptual skills with a variety of colored spoons, both transparent and opaque, on a light table. Display the provocation with some spoons set out on the board, or another contrasting work surface, to increase curiosity and get children started.

A Sense of Belonging

Early childhood is a significant period of development for children, including the emergence of new abilities in areas such as language and physical, psychosocial, and cognitive development, and the early childhood ecosystem greatly influences children's identity and development. Infants begin to recognize that they are separate beings from their primary caregivers. They notice differences and similarities between themselves and other people, thus developing the categorical self, which is another part of their identity. Children learn that even though they are separate and distinct from objects, entities, or other human beings, they are still part of their world. Children become aware of their age, height, gender, knowledge, capacities, and skills. As children with diverse abilities perceive and categorize the differences and similarities in Loose Parts, they make connections about their own differences and similarities with other children in their community. When children are accepted and respected, their self-esteem increases and forms the foundation for future relationships with others.

As relationships continue and children spend more time playing together, they acquire subjective feelings about their distinctiveness from others. They establish a sense of their individuality. Children also notice how other people perceive them and relate to them. Children with diverse abilities may be specifically sensitive and aware of how people react to their unique characteristics. That is why creating spaces where children of varying abilities are recognized and where they are in charge of their play and learning is so crucial.

Sarah uses glasses to help her eyes to align and function together. She often rejected them, and her family was concerned that her strabismus would deteriorate if she stopped using her glasses. They tried many strategies and talked to other families with children who used glasses. Sarah's family finally realized that her glasses were too big and that she was uncomfortable and self-conscious. They bought her a new pair of glasses, which helped her feel more comfortable with her identity. Fortunately, the children at her preschool are very respectful and do not tease her for wearing glasses. The educators make every effort to provide a safe space where Sarah sees herself represented. They have books with photos of children wearing glasses and have eyeglasses in the dramatic play area and other parts of the ecosystem. Playing with the plastic eyeglasses gives Sarah an understanding that her eyeglasses are part of who she is, and there is no shame in wearing them. Gaining a positive sense of identity and purpose has protected her against the stressors of eye surgeries and ongoing medical tests. This story shows how a supportive environment can help children create a sense of place and find purpose in their abilities.

Sarah's story is not unique. Many children enter early childhood programs figuring out who they are and how they fit in. Being accepted and creating a sense of self is even more difficult for children with diverse abilities because of societal messages and perceptions. Not only do they have to find commonalities with other children, but they frequently redefine their identity as they come to new understandings of their capacities. When children with diverse abilities attend an early childhood program where they are accepted and respected, they find ways to overcome challenges and become valued members of the community. As mentioned in other chapters, the affordances of Loose Parts allow children to find purpose in their play. For instance, Gabriel, a delightful and exuberant child who has Down syndrome, is loved and respected by all the children in his early childhood program. He finds profound joy in construction and is often seen outdoors stacking large wooden blocks. His construction continues indoors, where he builds tall structures. He climbs on the stepladder so he can reach the top of the tower. Educators Tomas and Daniela keep an eye on what Gabriel is doing, and they always come close when they see him climbing on the stepladder, but they do not stop him. They know that Gabriel has a sense of purpose and looks forward to accomplishing his goal. Gabriel regularly invites other children to join him in the building and, in his own way, gives them instructions on what to do. Gabriel is developing his identity as he builds relationships with children and adults. Since he entered the program and engaged in play, his cognitive, socioemotional, and physical development have advanced notably.

A sense of place builds a sense of belonging, acceptance, and respect for children's authentic ways of being in the world. When children feel safe to play, explore, create, design, and just be themselves, they trust the place and the people and objects within the space. As children with diverse abilities manipulate and move Loose Parts, they begin to trust their capacities and they know that the place they belong to is safe. When children are familiar with their community, they bond with the place. Finding pods and seeds on a walk helps children connect to the neighborhood. In Lincoln Community Preschool's neighborhood, peacocks roam freely. Children often pick up feathers and integrate them into their play. The children are learning to respect the flora and fauna of their community. Creating a sense of place takes time and intentionality, and it begins with the educators and their perceptions and assumptions. It requires that educators observe and reflect on their beliefs and practices. Take time to write down what you feel is special about your program and what sets you apart from other programs. Consider the following:

- How is your place/program special or unique?
- How did you create these special qualities?
- What would you like to do to make your program even more special?
- What steps would you need to take to make these ideas realistic goals?

- How do Loose Parts contribute to the children's sense of place?
- What inclusion strategies are you using to support children with diverse abilities?

Routines, rituals, and traditions help establish a sense of place for young children, and children with diverse abilities thrive under the consistency. These events let children repeat experiences and gain familiarity with one another and with the space. The routines and rituals of your program are important because they not only offer predictable experiences, but the traditions established help create history in your early childhood ecosystems. Children can look back and have fond memories of special events and interactions or remember the safe, predictable feeling of being well cared for.

The educator's role is to offer consistency, trust, rituals, and traditions that are inclusive and responsive to children with diverse abilities. Consider the daily, weekly, monthly, and yearly routines and rituals of your ecosystems. For example, throughout the school year, at Children's Circle Nursery School in Van Nuys, California, children find gemstones hidden by the educators. The children create rules about how many stones they can take home a week. They are learning that other children may want to take stones home, so taking only two stones a week is inclusive of other children. They are learning respect and how to be with one another in the communal space.

In many ways, infusing Loose Parts into the environment is a tradition, a ritual, and a routine. Children come to expect the open-ended play and the social interactions they develop as they construct and create together. They enjoy the freedom to express their authentic selves as they play with the Loose Parts and the other children. They also expect that new Loose Parts will be added to the environment to challenge their thinking. Loose Parts bring flexibility and consistency (I know, it may seem a contradictory concept) within the rituals and routines that exist in the ecosystem. They offer flexibility in the way the children use them and consistency as children become used to recognizing their own power over the objects. For example, as children arrive in the morning, they can walk around and find new Loose Parts invitations, inspirations, and provocations set up to engage them in play. They also know they have the freedom to move the Loose Parts to support their ideas and interests. Children with diverse abilities feel confident and know they can ask for help as they need it. When it is time to gather as a community to sing songs and tell stories, Loose Parts become an integral part of the process. Children bang on cans and pots and pans, dance with scarves and movement ribbons, and share stories of their play and what they created with the Loose Parts. Organizing and sorting Loose Parts becomes part of the cleaning routine. Loose Parts enhance yearly celebrations of the harvest, winter, and end of the school year.

A sense of place and belonging grows as children bond and develop secure attachments with peers and adults. This is crucial for children with diverse abilities. Consider how you help children in your program form secure attachments. What steps do you take to make children with diverse abilities and their families feel a sense of belonging? A sense of belonging doesn't just happen; it takes time and effort to foster. Focused, planned ideas are important.

Loose Parts can help you form strong connections with families. Take a photo of a Loose Part you want to collect. Invite families to help you collect them. Set a basket or a box at the entrance of the classroom to gather them. Participating in this simple community project helps children and families develop a sense of belonging. Provide a cubby or shelf where each family can display important artifacts that represent them, and invite them to share the objects' meanings. Consider adding dolls with diverse abilities as conversation starters for understanding others with diverse skills. Nurture a homelike atmosphere, including pillows and blankets, comfortable furniture, plants, and soft lighting. Allow for a level of messiness. Create spaces to display children's work and to revisit it as they need, to make sense of their thinking. Children need to know that not everything must be perfect. When children feel a part of the community, they are willing to contribute to maintaining the space. When children are acknowledged through compassionate in-person interaction as well as physical learning materials, they gain a secure sense of place.

Have baskets for Loose Parts that are alike yet different, such as three types of colorful boxes. This motivates children to categorize and notice differences.

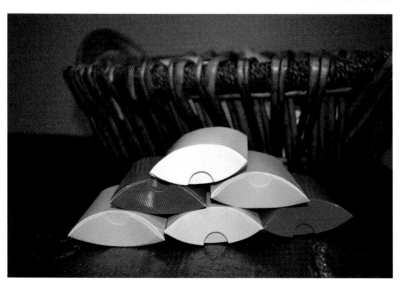

Playing with eyeglasses normalizes the use of various vision aids. The materials reduce stigma as they spur children to be curious, ask questions, and understand others with different sight and vision capacities. They can also be incorporated into dramatic play.

Children use found materials in their environment to generate their own games, such as nature tic-tac-toe. Giving children extended free time to invent their own games from items they collect can profoundly affect their sense of purpose.

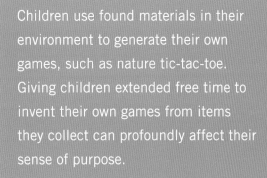

Emotions, Communication, and Collaboration

Emotions are real, and the ways they make us feel are also real. Children need adults to understand that they often have "big" feelings, and getting them under control takes time. A "big" feeling many times can be scary and challenging to understand. Learning to manage emotions takes time and profound understanding from the adults in charge. There is currently a movement in early childhood education to use emojis to help children express their feelings. My concern with this approach is how the emotions expressed with the emojis are insufficient and disconnected from children's real feelings. Children need more than an emoji to discern how they feel. This is particularly true for children with diverse abilities, who may have a difficult time self-regulating.

A more authentic way to explore feelings uses storytelling. Natural wood blocks combined with peg people help children express what they feel. Adding peg people that represent diverse abilities helps children see themselves represented. Storytelling helps adults talk about children's emotions with authenticity and empathy. When adults engage children in authentic conversations, they help them name their emotions. Listening to children as they play and tell stories using Loose Parts clues in educators to what children understand and know.

Documentation supports children in understanding and communicating their ideas, interests, and emotions. A story of the moment dictated by the child or captured by the educator provides a reminder of what happened. Displaying anecdotes, photos, and drawings throughout the environment helps children follow a sequence and revisit their investigations. As children study the photo, they see how other children view the same challenge. In this way, documentation helps children understand contextual information and can strengthen their abilities to understand different perspectives.

Including photographs of children demonstrating empathy and collaboration strengthens the message of what is valued in the classroom. The photos spur conversations that reiterate the importance of listening to and respecting one another. Children can use the photographs to sort and classify the different moments they see. Mount the photos on blocks or cardboard tubes to be used in storytelling and construction. For example, on a visit to Pacific Primary, a school located in San Francisco, I was intrigued by the colorful shipping tubes with photos of a child on each tube. I had asked the educator for permission to open one of the tubes to see what was inside. Ryder kept watching me. He looked at me and in a soft voice said, "You just did something very, very bad." I was confused but focused on rectifying what I did. Fortunately, the educator stepped in and said to Ryder, "I know that our agreement was to ask before we open someone else's tube. Miriam asked if she could see inside. Would you like to show her your tube?" Ryder got his tube from the shelf and showed me the message inside. He then explained that the message was what he wanted to do to help others. This simple idea helps children take ownership of their feelings and actions. It creates understanding and democracy. It is also an informal assessment of a student's ability to infer information and feelings from contextual clues, determining the extent of any social-skill challenges.

Recognizing people's emotions is crucial for building relationships. Children make inferences about other people's feelings and use the cues to make decisions about how they react in given circumstances. Learning to decipher other people's reactions helps children understand themselves, self-organize, and respond with empathy. Theory of mind, the ability to attribute mental states to ourselves and others, is a foundational element for social interaction. Developing theory of mind supports children to predict, interpret, and react to the behavior of others. Theory of mind starts to develop early in infancy and continues to develop through childhood. Eventually, having a theory of mind helps children predict what someone thinks or feels about what another person is thinking or feeling. They also begin to understand complex language that relies on the theory of mind, such as lies, sarcasm, and figurative language. Theory of mind develops as children interact with peers and adults. The more children engage in play, the more they understand different perspectives. In *Forming Ethical Identities in Early Childhood Play,* Brian Edmiston (2008) argues that over time, pretending to be other people assists children to take up other perspectives, to become responsible for their actions, and to respond to other people's feelings and actions.

Consider how symbolic and pretend play helps children develop a theory of mind and eventually perspective taking. Neal, Adriana, and Joaquin use scarves as capes to pretend to be superheroes. They re-create a sequence of events that Adriana experienced as she evacuated her home due to forest fires. As they play, they talk about their fears and feelings. They enact how they would get their dogs and cats out of their house. Adriana gets a basket and starts filling it with dolls, stuffed animals, scarves, and blankets. She says, "I have to take you with me because I can't let you be hurt." Neal approaches and gets another basket and starts adding acorns and a variety of pods. He says, "We will bring food so they can be okay. We are superheroes and we will take care of them." Joaquin, who has had a hard time understanding other people's feelings, joins Neal and Adriana and in a quiet voice says, "Adriana, don't be scared." The children are demonstrating their ability to recognize and understand other people's feelings.

While children with diverse abilities may play differently than their peers who are typically developing, play is still essential for building creativity, problem solving, and the spontaneous ability to form relationships. Creating community requires intentionality, planning collaborative opportunities, but also giving children independent quiet time. An environment set up to help children with diverse abilities must integrate areas to relax away from loud sounds and noise, areas to be fully active, and places for sensory-processing exploration. With careful observation and listening, adults can discern what triggers the "big" emotions and modify the surroundings to prevent dysregulation and to support children in gaining control. Loose Parts help children relax and learn to understand and control their emotions. Sand and water play is incredibly calming. Pillows and soft scarves provide a smooth surface to touch as children bring their feelings under control. If noisy and crowded situations cause anxiety, noise-canceling headphones may help. Placing these adaptations throughout the environment allows children to self-regulate their learning while meeting their own needs. An environment infused with Loose Parts where children with diverse abilities effectively function may require some extra structure. For example, when a child enjoys stacking metal washers of different sizes together, metal containers of different sizes invite the child to sort and classify by size. When setting up an invitation for transient art using glass beads, define the space to work with frames or bamboo plates so children know where to create their art. Other times, setting different surfaces for building engages children in further inquiry.

Engaging in conversation with children is a powerful way to learn more about their ideas and interests. For example, when educators observe children creating transient art using buttons, they may notice frustration building when things are not going as planned. At that point, educators can approach children and make a simple statement such as, "I know that sometimes when things are challenging, we can get frustrated. Let's think of a different approach to complete your work." Observe and listen intently to what children are doing and saying. Reflect on what you heard to show that you are listening and caring. For example, "I notice that you have been working for a long time to balance the driftwood and it keeps toppling over. That must make you feel frustrated." If you are correct, the children will feel validated. If you are not correct, they may tell you exactly what they're feeling. The key here is to know when to step in and when to let the moment pass. Intervening too early may affect the process of self-regulation. Waiting too long can make a situation escalate.

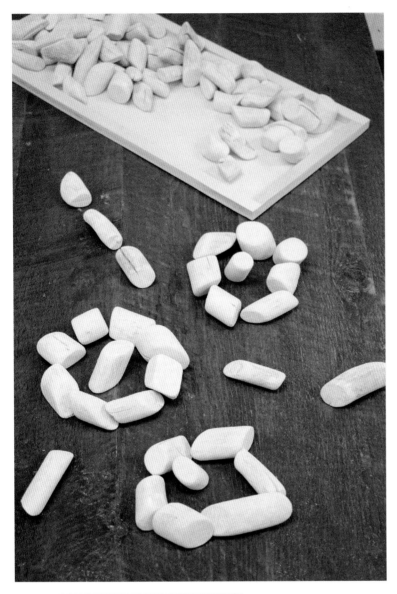

Children with diverse abilities use mini driftwood pieces to collaborate verbally and nonverbally. Irregular shapes challenge children to communicate as they balance, build, and invent with the wood.

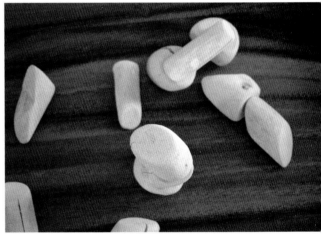

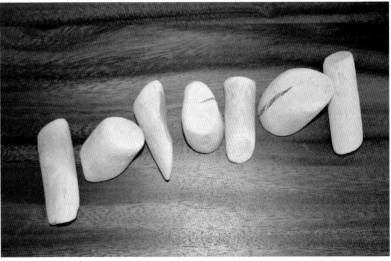

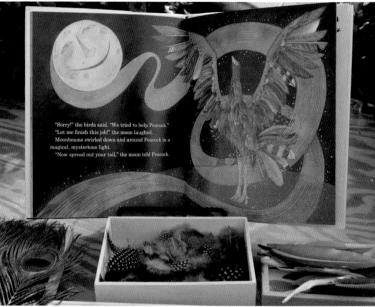

Soft feathers from the peacocks that live in their community are relevant and meaningful to the children. Providing a visual or tactile defined work boundary, such as a contrasting framed canvas, encourages children to work with Loose Parts with increased confidence.

Children can search for items like pine cones, pine needles, and flowers outdoors, or educators can bring nature into the ecosystem to allow children with diverse sensory abilities to explore items and their characteristics in their own way and in their own time. Ask questions about their selections and designs to encourage continued discovery.

An invitation with tubes on a pegboard and pebbles enhances collaborative play and group problem solving. Present the moldable tubes without prearranging them on the board to encourage children to collaborate in using the materials.

Children enter the flow of play as they make their own designs in Zen gardens, which engage the senses, boost creativity and cognition, and aid both children and adults in identifying and communicating emotions.

Chapter 6
Engaging Creativity

Young children exemplify creativity and creative thinking. They play with ideas, exploring and testing their hypotheses and theories with creativity. They are open to making mistakes and finding new possibilities within challenges. They have the incredible urge to create, and their joy in creative expression is cathartic, inclusive, and universal. Creativity allows children to consider alternatives and push beyond the constraints of fear and other limitations by generating innovative ways of thinking. Creativity helps them solve problems, explore, and comprehend the world in which we live. The educators' role is to create ecosystems that support, promote, and embrace creativity, and what better way than by exploring the multiple affordances that Loose Parts offer?

Children's brains need to acquire memory associations that link pleasure with learning. Loose Parts, combined with the creative arts, provide this link by connecting learning with the delights of innovative experiences and play. When we explore our childhood memories, we may recognize that our most significant and creative learning happened when we played with other children in the neighborhood. With my friends and neighbors, I explored the forest, empty fields, and parks in the community. Rocks became markers for a spontaneous ball game or formed the outline for hopscotch. Together we made small fairy houses out of sticks, grass, and flowers that we gathered. This was my favorite play. I climbed what seemed like tall boulders, and I felt like conquering the tallest mountain. I walked on a fence and felt like a tightrope walker. With my friends, I mixed potions, and we saw ourselves as chemists. The days seemed too short, and I woke up every morning feeling excited about what each new day would bring. One idea led to another, connecting into an ongoing chain propelled by my imagination, creativity, and play. As I played with my friends, I found joy in creating complex play sequences and made toys from tree branches, sticks, bottle caps, feathers, stones, chalk, string, glue, boxes, discarded pieces of fabric, and everything and anything we could find. I gathered with neighborhood friends to spontaneously cocreate dramatic play sequences that lasted for days. Other times, together we organized impromptu musical bands with homemade instruments. Everyone contributed. Our play was inclusive and sparked our imagination, creativity, and problem solving. Together we gained the skills necessary for cooperation, cocreativity, respect, social justice, and understanding. I often wonder if my creativity comes from these play experiences. I know that my childhood may seem idyllic and not the reality for many children and families. I think we must ask ourselves, "How do we create more opportunities for children to engage in inclusive free play?"

Unlocking the secrets of creativity has long been a motivator for scholars, scientists, psychologists, sociologists, and anthropologists. Several research studies are dedicated to the importance of creativity and how it influences learning and development. Some important research on creativity includes the works of E. P. Torrance, Teresa Amabile, and Mihaly Csikszentmihalyi, who each discovered that creativity emerges from our interest and curiosity and that everyone has the capacity to develop their creativity.

Creativity is a process that can be learned and supported. Like play, creativity is fluid and often messy. The process takes many forms, from conceiving an idea to shaping thoughts into something tangible to creating a work of art. As children create, they test and try new things; they are fascinated by the process of creation and not necessarily the final product. Creativity is an inoculation for boredom and failure. When the brain has reasons to expect that something previously enjoyable will soon happen, that expectation results in an increased release of the neurotransmitter dopamine, which increases pleasure and reduces stress. For example, three-year-old Ariana has sensory integration challenges. Her excitement is noticeable when she creates a new design at the light table. She discovers that light shines through the colorful acrylic tubes. That encourages her to keep testing new items to explore at the light table. She is engaged and relaxed in her play, and her brain is open to new ideas. When children expect pleasure when new Loose Parts are introduced, the release of this anticipatory dopamine frees them from self-predicted failure and expected boredom. They suspend judgment, leave competition behind, and embrace the possibilities that creativity and play offer.

When we focus on creativity instead of intelligence or achievement, we see children's strengths and possibilities for their future. Educators need to observe and recognize how creativity manifests in each child. Some children demonstrate creativity in their capacity to generate new ideas. Other children show creativity in their art, while others use their creative powers to construct, engineer, and apply scientific thinking. Some children have tremendous musical creativity. We must create cultures that value all children's creative capacities and provide them with varied possibilities to express them. Loose Parts have a fantastic ability to support creativity and promote original thinking. For example, Liam, a five-year-old with an ADHD diagnosis, is an incredibly creative engineer. His towers are elaborate, and he combines different types of blocks and other Loose Parts into his structures. Inspired by a book on stained glass windows, he uses transparent scarves to create a similar effect. His creativity allows him to focus, and when encouraged, he makes meaningful connections that will further his learning. We can say that Liam gets in the flow of play as defined by Csikszentmihalyi (2013).

Creativity fosters inquiry, new perspectives, independence, positivity, confidence, innovation, and ingenuity. Children with diverse abilities need creativity to thrive and discover their individual strengths. A child who has partial sight creates a beautiful sculpture using clay and glass beads. Meanwhile, a child with sensory integration challenges engages in a rhythmic musical interpretation using gourds as maracas. A young child with neurodiversity creates a striking collage with photographs and postcards. A child who is intellectually advanced draws an original weblike design that is both insightful and intricate, then re-creates it using blocks and natural Loose Parts. Each of these children with diverse abilities is stretching in different ways by engaging the mind, extending knowledge, and tapping into creativity. Continuously encouraging children to use their creativity to solve problems and create innovative products is vital. Loose Parts give children with diverse abilities extra encouragement; they maximize their strengths, talents, interests, energy, effort, and resilience.

All children, regardless of their physical, cognitive, social, and emotional developmental level, have individual interests, ideas, and capacities. Early in my career, I practiced as a vision therapist, and I worked every week with David, a five-year-old who had partial vision. I would bring a variety of Loose Parts (back then, I did not know they were Loose Parts) and introduce them one by one to David. I wanted him to explore and use his eyes to track the objects, many of which shone some sort of light to help him. Yet David was more interested in building blocks. I noticed how he followed the surface of each block. He carefully picked the shape he wanted to add to a structure. He got very close so that he could see what he was building. He described what he was doing and could name all the shapes. David was an incredibly creative builder and was curious enough to test the different blocks I brought him. He always found a way to pursue his creativity, and all he needed was enough adult support to keep his interest alive.

The visual arts promote creativity, and children with diverse abilities benefit from open-ended and process-oriented explorations. Creating transient art with Loose Parts lets children revisit their ideas, start them again, and design and redesign to their hearts' desire. Making art with Loose Parts encourages object manipulation, problem-solving skills, symbolic representation of ideas, and meaningful interaction with other children. Creativity grows through playful interactions, language stimulation, multisensory experiences, and ample opportunities for unstructured play and discovery, both individually and in collaboration with peers. Children benefit from exploring a range of Loose Parts that promote music, art, construction, movement, dance, and active engagement.

Children with diverse physical abilities may benefit from adapted positioning that supports them as they explore small Loose Parts. Silicone adaptive aids help them hold tools. Provide a tray to contain the Loose Parts, or use Velcro to attach an empty frame to the work space. Children who use wheelchairs or walkers need an appropriate-height table for the wheelchair to slide under or a high enough surface for them to work standing. Many children enjoy building on the surface of shelf units with different levels that add complexity to their play with Loose Parts. Include children with limited mobility in upper-body movement activities by giving them a ribbon streamer to hold or an instrument to play. To create inclusion and equity, provide enough adaptive equipment for all children to use regardless of ability.

Children with diverse speech and language abilities can work with other children to create a woven ribbon design or a collective mural using tiles. They benefit from talking about their artwork and sharing ideas with peers through conversation or pictorial representations. For example, Jamila is working on her language skills and uses small wooden Loose Parts to tell intricate stories that other children enjoy. One of my favorite activities is making shadow puppets to tell stories and express feelings and ideas. Children enjoy using flashlights and forming puppets with their hands. They also find different Loose Parts to represent animals, trees, or buildings. Add more concrete objects to the Loose Parts collection so that children have a tangible way to share what they are thinking.

Adding Loose Parts to different classroom areas engages children who are hesitant to share their ideas verbally. For instance, Luis is beginning to speak English, and he listens to and observes what other children say and do as they use Loose Parts for cooking. He waits until he knows a word and feels ready to share it with other children.

Children with neurodiversity have individual ways of exploring and perceiving the environment. Some children enjoy visually driven activities, such as matching loose rocks to a book or matching cards, re-creating works of art using tiles, or looking at photographs and re-creating what they see using blocks. Other children prefer tactile experiences such as finding acrylic letters in a tub of water beads. Placing fidgets throughout the classroom and encouraging their use can help children to relax and self-regulate.

Children benefit from the gift of time. Creativity takes time as well as the ability to stay focused and engaged. Having time for self-initiated play helps develop focus and motivation. Time is particularly important for children experiencing developmental delays. Flexible schedules that offer extended time support children's creativity. Sometimes children need an adult or a peer to break down an exploration and guide them on using a specific tool. Educators can use the time in a flexible schedule to model for children how things work and show some of the affordances of Loose Parts. For example, Janelle has shown Melinda how to use adaptive tongs to pick up silicone beads and jingle bells. Together they are working on using regular tongs. It is impressive to see Janelle's understanding and compassion as she guides Melinda. Janelle also benefits by learning about Melinda. Having lots of time to play together has cemented their relationship.

An inclusive ecosystem helps children find creativity within challenges and limitations. Support children to value their creative spirit and to challenge their thinking about their limitations, including misconceptions about their abilities and capacities. Building on children's strengths instead of focusing only on their needs helps educators recognize that children are creative and capable of imagining positive outcomes, rather than often failing to achieve a goal.

Key Reflections

- How do you see children expressing their creativity as they play with Loose Parts?
- What Loose Parts and materials captivate their interest?
- Where else in the ecosystem can you add Loose Parts to support children's creativity?

The Car Needs Gas

Madison and Ryder worked alongside one another to align the vehicles at the "gas station." The curved tube provided a child-sized handheld "gas pump" to fill and refill the "tanks" on the vehicles. The children cheered with excitement with each gas filling and lined up vehicles to take turns and wait at the pump. Additional vehicles were added and subtracted as the children saw fit. Other children using vehicles in other areas of the play yard made their way over to the pump station to fill their tanks, then resumed their play at their original location.

—Casey Johnson, Lincoln Community Preschool

Egg-shaped crayons, faceted crayons, and thick triangle markers and crayons provide additional input to the fingers and palm of the hand, developing children's grasp on writing implements as well as supporting fine-motor control while scribbling and drawing. Use medium- or regular-thickness crayons as an increased challenge for children with higher-level fine-motor skills. Incorporating uneven wood stones adds interest to the provocation, inspires creativity, and enhances observational skills.

Cookie cutters in the snow create transient art impressions. These tools can be used in so many ways—depending on children's strength, cookie cutters can be pressed into clay for increased resistance or dipped in paint to make prints.

Photo Credit: Alexis Baran

Weaving colorful shoelaces in a wire frame is an introductory visual arts activity. (Ensure that the holes are wide enough for regular laces.) For children developing fine-motor coordination and pincer grasp, attach a stiff or lengthened component to one end of the lacing material.

The Visual Arts—An Expression of Hope

The visual arts are an integral part of early childhood education. Ecosystems that promote the visual arts enhance children's artistic development and nurture an appreciation for aesthetics and beauty. Art experiences help children to find meaning in themselves and their world. The visual arts enrich all children's lives, not just a talented few (Isbell and Raines 2013) and bring balance to children's lives, acting as an equalizer that crosses cultures and societal boundaries. They provide children an expression of hope and healing and make them feel included and welcome. Children with diverse abilities reenvision their abilities and talents simply by using the creative process. When children engage in process-oriented art, they gain power over their capacities and ultimately gain understanding and knowledge that will positively influence their future academic outcomes. To illustrate, Josiah gravitates toward the art space. He picks up the basket with glass beads and brings them to the long table. He starts to line up the beads at the edge of the table. When there are no more beads in the baskets, he walks back to the shelf and looks at the items in the different baskets. He then notices the frames. He brings them back to the table and proceeds to fill the edges of the frames with the glass beads. Josiah is still not able to communicate verbally, but his actions tell us what he is thinking. Once he fills the frames, he puts the beads back in the basket and takes the frames to the shelf. His interest in exploring space is seen in his drawings as well. He often starts with a large circle and fills it with smaller circles. The educators have noticed his interest in exploring how items occupy space and are constantly looking for other Loose Parts to bring into the environment.

Like all children, those with diverse abilities have an intrinsic need to communicate and let others know how they feel, what they think, and who they are. With the visual arts, children with diverse abilities can explore their creativity, ideas, and interests in their own way without judgment or achievement expectations. Furthermore, the visual arts give children a sense of accomplishment so they see themselves as creative, contributing members of the classroom community. Art provides children with diverse abilities a way to express their emotions creatively and extend their communication skills, encouraging socialization. Art gives them an outlet for emotions ranging from anger and fear to joy and love. It develops children's appreciation for creating art and valuing collaborative results and shared experiences.

Critically, the visual arts also develop visual thinking abilities. Visual thinking organizes thoughts and improves the ability to think and communicate. It conveys complex or potentially confusing information. It helps children connect thoughts and ideas as they draw, design with Loose Parts, and engage in dramatic play or storytelling. Loose Parts help children bring out their internal thinking processes, making them more transparent, explicit, and actionable. When children can draw or represent their ideas, they can also implement them and follow up on their goals, thus bringing hope and increasing self-esteem. Imagine Ariadna as she uses wooden cardholders, geometric wooden blocks, and peg people to create a carousel. She is communicating what she did over the weekend. Ariadna is beginning to develop oral language, and these expressions of her thinking are priceless to her and her family.

The visual arts are a communication system that helps children express themselves in other language forms. This system of symbols emerges from their drawing, imaginative play, and other artistic endeavors. Drawing and mark making are some of the first representations young children create. You may notice that as children play with Loose Parts, they will use them in a way that connects to mark making. For instance, Aaron writes his name using sticks, and Jennifer uses craft sticks to create the shape of a house and a tree. As children grow in their mark making and Loose Parts play, they expand the multitude of languages they can use to express their thinking.

Art serves as a catalyst that supports perceptual and conceptual learning. Perceptual learning is the process of how our sensory systems respond to stimuli and how knowledge grows through experience. Conceptual learning is how children organize information in logical mental structures. For example, Simone, Arminta, and Lucas start lining up rose pine cones in a line. They take turns placing the pine cones. At one point, Simone and Lucas step back and Simone says, "We need to add other things to fill the space. We are running out of pine cones." Arminta, who has aphasia caused by a mild brain injury, listens carefully to the conversation. Simone and Lucas plan how to complete their art, and they periodically stop and ask for Arminta's ideas. Together they decide to find more natural materials. In a whisper, Arminta says, "I think we need baskets to bring nature here." Simone understands what Arminta means and replies, "Yeah, the baskets will help us bring more wood pieces so we can finish our art." Simone and Lucas are helping Arminta develop conceptual understanding and learning.

The visual arts encourage risk-taking instead of conformity. Children make sense of the world as they access intentionally planned visual arts explorations. The following are just a few ways children can explore the visual arts to design, create, and innovate using Loose Parts.

The Power of Printmaking

We are surrounded by print, from cereal boxes to books to advertisements. Simple stamp printing in the sand allows children to explore cause and effect, pattern making, positive and negative space, shape, and line. The hands-on nature of printmaking naturally nurtures children's capability to manipulate materials. In printmaking, children have a direct connection to their work, and they can see their creations magically unfold before them. Children can use Loose Parts to explore printing in the sand or mud. Incorporating other art media expands children's understanding of print, making relief prints, rubbings, and monoprint and using Loose Parts to print on paper and other surfaces. Printmaking helps children see themselves as powerful artists who leave a mark in the world. It strengthens their creative spirit and helps them understand that things change but are still beautiful.

The Inviting Qualities of Clay

Working with clay is liberating and exciting. Its malleable qualities make it ideal for manipulating and for exploring texture. Working it also releases stress and tension. Children can imprint, stretch, roll, and transform to create anything their imagination dictates. When children work with clay, they get in the flow and enjoy the moment. Clay provides clear opportunities for children to learn about the functional aspects of art, the expressive potentials of art, and the importance of the design process. Placing containers of Loose Parts close to the clay table invites children to enhance their clay designs. For children with diverse abilities, clay is an incredible tool for strengthening muscles, aiding sensory integration, and facilitating communication, self-esteem, and self-expression. For instance, Tyron needs a lot of stimulation to integrate his senses. When you observe him working with natural clay, you can see how he brings a ball of it to his nose to smell. He carefully pinches the edges of the ball and uses his thumb to indent a hole, forming a saucerlike structure. He stops and looks around the area, notices a container with beautiful glass beads, and adds them to the vessel. He presses hard and makes sure they stay in place. Once he finishes, he walks to Vanesa, the educator, and places the clay in her hand. He points to the shelf and asks, "Can you put up there? I want to give to Mom." He then runs off and starts working on another clay sculpture.

The Excitement of Construction

When children build with wooden blocks, mini tree stumps, wood stones, or acrylic blocks, they become the architects of their own expression. Through this constructive strand of the visual arts, children learn about how things are made, how they work, how they balance, how they fit together, and how they support one another. As children construct, they realize how some items enhance their work and others distract from it. For example, different sizes and shapes of blocks can help with construction, but adding beads can distract from the construction process because they serve more of a decorative purpose.

Children use construction as a form of personal expression. They also make important connections from the two-dimensional form to the three-dimensional form. Construction is particularly suited for group work and also enhances

mathematical and scientific thinking. Children who have visual limitations explore Loose Parts with their hands to learn about their shape, size, texture, weight, and other characteristics. Wooden blocks covered with corrugated cardboard can facilitate building for children with diverse abilities. Take Billy, a five-year-old with limited vision who enjoys building and is often seen with other children in the block area. When Billy first demonstrated an interest in construction, educator Sean spent time familiarizing Billy with the blocks and Loose Parts in the construction zone. Sean encouraged Billy to feel the blocks and Loose Parts and describe what he felt. Sean's comments and questions helped Billy become aware of the Loose Parts and the blocks' basic traits. For example, Sean said, "That block is curved. Feel the curve. Touch this block. What do you notice?" Sean invites other children to join the exchanges with Billy, supporting Billy's social development. As children join the construction process, they support Billy as they engage in conversation: "Here, Billy, you need more stumps to create the tower for the castle." By engaging in the conversations, Billy feels part of the group and is open to further communication and conversations. Children with diverse abilities learn a lot about problem solving by trying out their own ideas, watching and listening to other children solve problems and adapt those ideas, and working with others to arrive at solutions. Adults can actively encourage children with diverse abilities to share ideas and work with others.

The Textures of Fabric and Fiber

Children explore the world through their senses, and incorporating textiles as Loose Parts into the environment further supports their sensory explorations. Fabrics and textiles support children's creative and representation capacities: children may weave, sew, classify, collage, build forts, and more. When children explore textiles, they learn about the structure of fabrics and fibers and how they are made. Children with diverse abilities may experience textiles and fabrics differently. For example, Marina is a four-year-old who is extremely sensitive to the cloth she wears. The textiles she touches need to feel pleasant to her. Even her socks need to be of certain fabric or she experiences self-regulation difficulties. In contrast, Lucas has a need to touch everything. He pokes, strokes, pulls, and touches every item he can. Then there is Ismael, who seems unaware of the surfaces or textiles in the environment. He may feel a rough sanding paper and not have a reaction. Intentionally integrating textile Loose Parts into the environment can have therapeutic results. Natural, smooth, and soft-textured fabrics added into the environment as Loose Parts may attract the interest of children who are more resistant to touch. For example, Marina may be comfortable using soft yarn to weave in a loom. She may also accept textiles that have been glued onto wooden blocks. Ribbons, corduroy fabric, carpet squares, fabric samples, and yarn in sensory bins can support Lucas's interest in touching and feeling a range of textures. Ismael can benefit from encountering different textures, and he may be more interested in walking on different surfaces than touching items with his hands.

Art is a highly symbolic activity, a form of both cognitive and individual expression (Seefeldt 1995). Producing art requires children to think of an experience, idea, or feeling and construct symbols to represent or express what they know. The more opportunities we offer children with diverse abilities to represent their ideas and thinking by using Loose Parts and other art media, the more they will be able to understand themselves and communicate with others.

Select aesthetically engaging materials to pique children's interest in the visual arts. These acrylic blocks used for making pens on a lathe have mesmerizing sheens and designs. Children visually explore them or build structures that experiment with positive and negative space.

Children explore texture as they print clay using rolling pins with leaves as well as engraved pins. Provide a sponge in water for children to undo and redo their creations. Children who are developing tolerance for tactile input can use paintbrushes and rolling pins to experience the clay's properties.

Designing mandalas offers firsthand experience with art composition elements like pattern, repetition, rhythm, variety, unity, proportion, and scale. Creating such artwork complements executive functioning skills like working memory and planning. Open-ended target-shaped templates can assist students who are working on their visual-spatial skills in designing freely.

Uncomplicated provocations increase visual attention and focus and invite children to use the material in the manner they choose. Firm natural clay can be challenging for young children to tear, so providing pieces of various sizes allows children with different levels of manual strength to play independently.

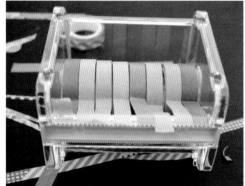

Children create washi tape artwork pieces by cutting and taping pieces on paper. Use thicker bands and set out fewer rolls for children working on pressure grading or fine-motor skills and for those who thrive with fewer available materials. Use a tape dispenser to assist children with peeling the rolls.

The Importance of Storytelling

Many of us have fond memories of being read to or listening to our family tell stories. My first memory was when I was five years old and my mother read the book *Heidi* to me. I remember her making the sounds from the book come alive as she read, such as the wind blowing in Heidi's bedroom and her different voices, like when she read passages that include Heidi's grandfather. I remember feeling sadness when we had to stop and anticipating when she could read to me again. I also have powerful memories of the stories shared by my father. He would not read from a book, but he shared some of his adventures as a child (many times they included things we should not do!). I can still see his face and hear his laughter as he told his stories. This is the power of storytelling. It connects us to family, community, and the earth we inhabit.

Storytelling has served as a vehicle for communication since the beginning of time. It is the oldest form of teaching and building community. Fundamentally, storytelling is the art of orally transmitting the tales shared by people and families. Storytelling helps bond people together and provides answers to questions about life. Stories define us, shape us, and help us imagine a hopeful future. Children are natural storytellers. They do not need to know how to read to tell stories. They just need an audience willing to listen. Stories create a sense of wonder about children's own lives and increase their curiosity about one another. Through storytelling, children learn to respect and appreciate diverse cultures and people who experience life differently. Loose Parts add another dimension by bringing a multisensory approach to storytelling and make the experience more inclusive for children with diverse abilities. Invite children to tell the story from a book or fairy tale shared in the classroom using Loose Parts. Add wire and metal circles when reading *Galimoto* by Karen Lynn Williams or set out baskets with small boxes when reading *Not a Box* by Antoinette Portis.

Stories are threaded throughout children's daily lives, from sharing what happened at school to telling about a moment that made them laugh. Children are powerful storytellers, and they take every opportunity to find an audience for their fables. In her book *The Boy Who Would Be a Helicopter*, author Vivian Gussin Paley (1990) shares the power stories have in the classroom, explaining that children are born knowing how to put their thoughts and feelings into account. As they engage in role play, children put their stories into action, as storytelling is theatrical play in a narrative form. Stories are also a powerful tool for healing. Immediately after the World Trade Center was attacked in 2001, I spent many hours at a child development center. Children told the story of the towers over and over—not directly, but in their play. They built tall block structures and ran through them to knock them down. Other times they asked educators to make paper airplanes to crash into their towers. This play went on for at least a month. Eventually, the children moved on to other play and told their stories in different ways.

When children are allowed to tell their stories, we open a space to share who they are, what they think, and what values guide them. Storytelling helps educators navigate intercultural misunderstandings and cultural insensitivities in the classroom. Children with diverse abilities can fully participate in storytelling, and Loose Parts are wonderful supports: shaking filled gourds simulates rain, pebbles in cans simulate thunder, and scarves serve as wings, capes, and dresses. For instance, Aziel has limited use of oral language, but he is incredibly expressive, using storytelling stones (stones that have drawings or stickers representing different objects) and wooden cutouts to share his complex stories with other children. Using concrete visual cues, designed into Loose Parts, children with diverse abilities share their knowledge, thoughts, and ideas. Storytelling playscapes further support children in telling their stories—and developing language skills—with felt animals and a variety of natural Loose Parts. As children with diverse abilities tell stories, they enhance their emotional development while promoting their social, cultural, and ethical identities.

Engaging children in storytelling has many benefits:

- **Enhancing speech and language:** When children tell stories, their vocabulary increases and their grammar improves.
- **Promoting critical thinking:** When children listen to and tell stories, their brains predict and plan what happens next. Their imaginations are sparked, and they can go beyond the words written in a book. Children learn that sometimes a story takes more than one day to tell. Loose Parts let children revisit, change, and grow their stories.
- **Encouraging the imagination:** When children tell stories, even when they retell familiar fairy tales, they take an imaginative and innovative approach, making parts of the story more exciting or telling a new ending.
- **Supporting comprehension:** Children repeat stories to understand their meaning and purpose. By listening to the story children share, you will know how children have comprehended the situations, emotions, and characters. The more stories children tell, the more their power to grasp, understand, and comprehend improves.
- **Increasing memory:** As children tell stories, they memorize details and sequences. Through recall, storytelling supports working memory and short-term and long-term memory.
- **Boosting self-confidence:** Children enjoy telling stories, and they are skilled storytellers. They feel confident when adults listen with interest and thrive when they tell a story to their peers.

- **Engaging children in collaboration:** Children learn about one another and eventually tell stories together. For instance, Gerardo and Jamila tell the story of a visit to the beach together with their families. They use shells and small driftwood pieces in the sand table.
- **Developing a love for books:** Children learn that books have stories just like theirs. They listen for the message in the books and understand the connection between oral and written language.
- **Developing expressive capacities:** When children tell a story, they slowly learn how to use their voices (tone, pitch, pause, volume, voice throw) and facial expressions, making them more eloquent. They also learn to judge others' emotions by looking at their faces.

Gail de Vos, Merle Harris, and Celia Barker Lottridge (1995), authors of *Telling Tales: Storytelling in the Family,* suggest that storytelling allows children with diverse abilities to participate in experiences that are uniquely human. Whether children manipulate Loose Parts to create Storytelling Playscapes, use storytelling sticks or storytelling stones, wear scarves as capes, wave sticks as swords, pretend to eat small pine cones as food, or dance with ribbons to act out stories, we must recognize that the process brings equity and inclusion into the classroom.

These figures do not look like specific animals, so through creative storytelling they can become most any animal a child wants! Precisely inserting flowers and leaves using the fingertips and efficient eye-hand coordination develops fine-motor and visual-motor integration skills. The natural materials also support revisiting ideas through the seasons.

An array of concrete items such as animals, fairies, trees, and buildings combined with Loose Parts provides endless creative storytelling opportunities. For children developing decision-making skills or who thrive with fewer choices, limit the pieces to a few of each type. Painting and drawing their own representations on wooden blocks can ignite children's storytelling.

Involve children in choosing which items to place stickers on, such as tree cookies, wood chips, sticks, or rocks, and allow them to pick out and place the stickers. To minimize visual input, display one item type at a time or use fewer items. As needed, assist children by starting a story (such as "I rode my bike today to . . .") and laying out a corresponding item.

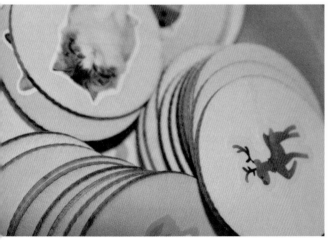

The tactile wooden pieces and contrasting black workspace enhance storytelling for children with diverse abilities. Allow children who are developing abstract thinking to simply explore the pieces or create an artful design. They may be beginning to tell their story in their own way.

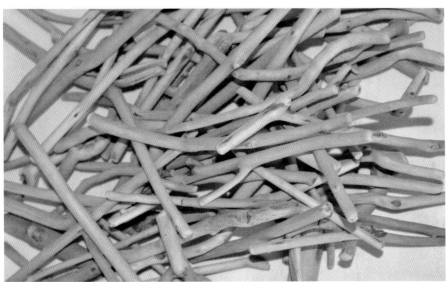

For children who are developing more abstract thinking and for those highly motivated by hands-on experiences, incorporate Loose Parts that are relevant to specific books. The three-dimensional representation brings two-dimensional pictures and ideas to life and allows for a richer interaction with the content.

Play and Creativity

Nothing promotes creativity better than play. We know play is essential to children's growth and development. The need to play is innate, and it drives children's ability to design and plan their own learning. Take a moment to consider how a diverse ability can affect how children engage in play. For example, Daniel presents with neurodiversity. He engages in play through repetition. We often see him building the same tower over and over. He seldom engages in dramatic play, and when he does, it is a repetitive cooking motion. Sammy is full of energy and very willing to participate in all types of play but finds it challenging to stay focused. Jazmine uses a walker to move around the classroom and struggles with accessing different areas. Jamal is in and out of the hospital when he experiences severe asthma and other ongoing health challenges. He loves to play with a variety of Loose Parts whenever he can, but the hygiene requirements in the hospital make it challenging to encourage the play he enjoys. The challenges presented in the stories may differ, but they all influence how children with diverse abilities engage in play.

Educators, families, and child life specialists must be creative and intentional when selecting Loose Parts and seek a variety of ways to engage in play with young children with diverse abilities. The following is an overview of the most common types of play identified in early childhood education (ages zero to eight) and some strategies that can help children with diverse abilities share ideas and embrace Loose Parts play.

Motor Play

In motor play, children use their bodies to perform spontaneous physical actions. For example, twenty-four-month-old Alona walks from one pillow to the next in the classroom. She crawls under the table and comes out on the other side, improvising an obstacle course. She stands up holding on to a table and walks slowly to the educator, Raya, who is sitting close by. She holds Raya's hands and smiles. It is important to note that until very recently Alona was not standing or walking—she moved and interacted with the ecosystem by crawling. Motor play contributes to development and learning, and it promotes healthy physical growth and maturation. Motor play is particularly important for children with physically challenging conditions. It strengthens their core and both gross- and fine-motor skills. Loose Parts such as planks, tree stumps, large blocks, river rocks, and other natural materials that invite running, jumping, and climbing add to the complexity of play in the outdoor ecosystem. When children stretch to reach a small rock or other Loose Part, they strengthen their core muscles while refining their grip.

Motor play is active and includes rough-and-tumble play, which is particularly important for children who have extra energy or decreased awareness of physical boundaries. In rough-and-tumble play, children climb over one another, wrestle, roll around, and even pretend to fight. This type of play is a basic human instinct that helps children develop many skills—and they are having fun!

Rough play helps young children do the following:

- understand the limits of their strength
- explore spatial relationships surrounding their changing positions in space
- test boundaries, including their limits and limits of other children
- negotiate what is acceptable for themselves and other children

Adults may perceive some of this play as aggressive, but when we observe children closely, we notice no fighting or mean intention in their actions. Simple changes in the environment increase safety for this type of play. For example, add ropes so children can spontaneously engage in tug-of-war. Rolled-up newspapers made into long "swords" allow children to fence with one another. Setting mats outdoors invites children to roll or wrestle. All these activities can be executed safely, and they truly help children with diverse abilities gain deeper understanding of their capacities.

Exploratory Play

In exploratory play, children use their senses to learn about the function and texture of the world around them. It starts at birth as infants adapt to their ecosystem and begin using their senses. They use hearing to recognize voices and use sight to find familiar faces. They use their sense of taste when they mouth their hands and when they suck while feeding. They explore textures when they pick up soft or hard Loose Parts or walk on different surfaces. When children use all their senses, they strengthen connections in their brains, leading to robust learning. Take Jacob, an active three-year-old who demonstrates early signs of neurodiversity. Water, water beads, and sand play soothe him. Sensory exploration appears to be an essential way he approaches the world. The educators notice how transitioning indoors is difficult for Jacob, so they discuss accommodations and decide they will keep the sand table available all day and give Jacob more opportunities for sensory exploration. They place baskets with rug samples in the quiet spaces. Tubs with jingle bells are available for Jacob to shake and listen to. The educators add shells and small rocks to the sand table. They also observe if the sensory stimulation is overwhelming to Jacob or other children and intentionally replace items.

Support children in exploratory play by creating a treasure basket. In 2002 Elinor Goldschmied introduced the concept of treasure baskets filled with intriguing objects to engage children in exploring objects at their leisure. Goldschmied's consultancy focused on the well-being and learning of infants in group care. She promoted the treasure basket as an essential strategy to support curiosity and concentration, the basis of all learning and creativity. Using treasure baskets with Loose Parts helps children feel ownership over the exploration. Treasure baskets can be curated to meet the interests and needs of individual children. They can be adapted for children who are hospitalized by including items that are easily cleaned and disinfected, and objects can be selected to engage children who have specific sensory interests. During the COVID-19 pandemic, treasure baskets helped classrooms adhere to physical distancing guidelines while supporting children's play. Observation will guide educators in deciding which Loose Parts to include in the baskets. As children become familiar with the objects, introduce a new Loose Part to create novelty and renew interest.

Functional Play

Functional play involves manipulating objects to discover specific functions. Children order, move, classify, connect, and screw items together to gain fluency in their uses. Functional play has a specific purpose that goes beyond exploration for exploration's sake. This type of play is often solitary, but when enough Loose Parts are involved, it may become cooperative. Functional play happens when Loose Parts or objects are used according to their intended function, as in rolling a ball, stacking blocks, connecting nuts with bolts, or pushing a car up and down a ramp. Functional play may also be defined as the conventional association of two or more things. For example, a child takes a spoon to feed a doll or picks up and throws a ball, expecting another child to catch it. Psychologist Sara Smilansky (2016) describes functional play as children using repetition in physical actions, language, and manipulation of objects based on their need for physical activity. Functional play precedes and supports the development of constructive and dramatic play.

Children with diverse abilities sometimes need support for functional play. Some have difficulty thinking flexibly because of organization, processing, or anxiety issues. Children with diverse abilities may prefer to focus on only one Loose Part at a time or choose to move from Loose Part to Loose Part without discovering the function and affordances of the objects. For instance, four-year-old Tonya, who has limited peripheral vision, enjoys moving small items around. She laughs when she hears the noise pebbles make as she shakes them inside a tin can. She uses a funnel-ended spoon to move jingle bells from one box to another. The sound guides her exploration. Her small-muscle dexterity is incredible, and she can assemble small beads onto strings to create necklaces. The educators have noticed that Tonya focuses only on items that are placed in front of her and ignores items in the periphery. They know that this is due to Tonya's vision, so with help from the vision therapist, they use Loose Parts to encourage her to focus her attention around the ecosystem. They combine colorful objects and place them next to the light table, one of Tonya's favorite places. They attract her attention by using their voices or shaking items. Little by little, Tonya learns to move her head to scan around her and notice other items. Her play and social interactions grow, and Tonya becomes more interested in exploring new items.

Educators, families, and child life specialists can observe and notice how children engage in functional play. Do the children use the Loose Part specifically for what it was designed, or do they use it in more abstract ways? How do children react to different Loose Parts? As you find answers to these questions, you can plan more intentionally to engage children with diverse abilities. One strategy to support children in play is to join them in what they are doing. Imitate how they play with the Loose Parts and add another possible way to use the item. For example, if the child is lining up tiles, start your own line of tiles. Step back and then add one tile on top of another tile. Notice how the child reacts and continue to stack the tiles. The intention is that eventually the child will imitate and build upon what you are doing.

Cause-and-Effect Play

Children drop balls to see if they bounce. They stack blocks to test when they topple over. Cause-and-effect play gives children a sense of control over their play while increasing their knowledge of the power and consequences of their actions. Often children with diverse abilities learn the cause and effect of Loose Parts independently. However, at times they need some support. Observe and notice how children interact with the Loose Parts. Design spaces that encourage them to see how Loose Parts offer a variety of affordances. For example, set out a water table with Loose Parts that either sink or float. Hide rocks in the sand area for children to dig out. Provide rubber bands, scrunchies, and zip ties for children to study the cause and effect of connecting and disconnecting Loose Parts.

Pretend Play and Sociodramatic Play

Pretend play supports children in developing the social skills they need to interact with other people in society and to understand the rules guiding the interactions. Children create imaginary realities that help them understand their real-life experiences. In imaginative play, children transform themselves or pretend to be different people or animals. Children use objects to express their ideas and imagination and carry out complex make-believe roles and situations. In imaginary play, children act out imaginary situations and stories, become different characters, and pretend they are in different locations and times. Examples of this type of play include make-believing a tree stump is a car, pretending to be a superhero with a scarf as a cape, and imagining a box as a sailing boat.

Sociodramatic play requires the use of imagination and the ability to think in abstract terms. These specific developmental skills start to emerge around two years of age. However, children with diverse abilities may take longer to develop the ability to engage in sociodramatic play. Children with diverse disabilities may engage in pretend play more simply. For instance, they may start by pretending to drink from a cup or hold and rock a doll. An illustration: Trevor is the father of Sean, a four-year-old with Down syndrome. Sean's family uses imaginative play to increase his communication and adaptive skills. Trevor picks up a doll and takes a cup from the shelf. He starts to bring the cup to the doll's mouth and watches to see Sean's reaction. Sean often repeats the behavior of bringing a cup to his mouth. Trevor says, "We are drinking water from a cup" and continues to hold the doll while bringing the cup to its mouth. Sean says in a loud voice, "My cup," identifying the symbol "cup" with the word. This skill demonstrates an understanding of possession and the knowledge that "I am a separate person with my own needs." The words and concepts are becoming the child's own, ready for spontaneous use. The more Sean engages in pretend play, the more he can follow and initiate increasingly complex and abstract play sequences. Later in the week, Sean holds the doll, this time using a plastic tube to simulate a bottle. Sean has now moved into more complex play and is using symbols to represent concrete ideas. Pretend play helps children with diverse abilities organize their external prompts and increases their flexibility and spontaneous engagement. With continued support and exposure, they will express their creativity and thinking through sociodramatic play. Using their new thinking and communicating skills to master these more advanced challenges gives children a lifelong capacity to cope and learn (Greenspan, Wieder, and Simons 1998).

Sociodramatic play gives children with diverse abilities the opportunity to showcase and explore their talents, inspiring them to be storytellers, actors, communicators, innovators, and creators. There is no doubt that Loose Parts play increases children's creativity, supports their social and emotional development, and makes them feel they belong to the classroom community. The following are steps children with diverse abilities may follow as they become more skillful in sociodramatic play.

1. **Imitative play:** Children undertake make-believe roles and express their thinking as they act out their pretend characters. For example, Solange picks up a spoon and moves acorns around a cooking pot while saying, "I am cooking like Mom." Design spaces where children can play together so children with diverse abilities emulate and learn from their peers.

2. **Make-believe with Loose Parts:** Children substitute Loose Parts for real objects. For instance, David picks up a long stick and says, "I am riding my pony." Join children in play and introduce new Loose Parts by pretending they are real objects, like driving a car using a round pizza tray or banging a metal pot as a drum.

3. **Verbal make-believe:** Children narrate what they are pretending in combination with body movements. For example, children describe what they are doing as they "shop," using metal washers as coins.

4. **Role playing:** Children reach an advanced level of sociodramatic play when they can sustain a role-play episode for at least ten minutes, such as when Janine takes turns with Aaron as they pretend to be construction workers.

Once children participate in pretend actions, support their imagination by adding more Loose Parts. Select Loose Parts that invite abstract and concrete thinking and add complexity as you see more sociodramatic play moments emerging.

Social Play

Social play is identified by the interaction among children as they plan, organize, and share a play sequence. During social play, children learn how to work together, communicate with peers, take turns, and engage in perspective taking. As children with diverse abilities become more skillful at playing, they begin to play with others. At times children with diverse abilities take longer to join social play. They may need extra time to make sense of the abstract and symbolic representations, rules, and meaning of the interactions. Other times children with diverse abilities need adult support to join social play interactions. Educators can create small-group opportunities to include children who benefit from extra time to warm up or recruit another child to engage the child with diverse abilities in play. The presence of a warm, responsive educator during play also helps children with diverse abilities feel safe and more willing to join in. The educator can help children with diverse abilities learn to read social cues, body language, and facial expressions so that they understand how their interactions affect others. Educators must create an ecology of respect so all children are aware of their role in including everyone. To illustrate: Addie, Antoine, and Jerome are playing a game of hot lava. They have arranged wooden planks on top of tree stumps and are walking around, balancing on the planks. Lucia, who uses a walker, wants to join the game. The children's first reaction is to say, "You can't play because if you fall the lava will kill you." Addie stops and gets off the planks, carefully walking on the side that has no lava. She approaches Lucia, looks up at Antoine and Jerome, and says, "Come on, guys, we need Lucia to come with us. We have to find a way to protect her." The play shifts into creating a way to keep Lucia from falling into the lava. They plan, construct, and test different ideas. Lucia contributes, laughing with enjoyment. They never find a full solution, but they build bonds based on empathy through their collaborative play that last all year.

Construction Play

In construction play, children build with three-dimensional objects, manipulating items to create something new by stacking, assembling, connecting, and disconnecting. Children work toward a goal or product of their choosing—creating a mandala using glass beads, making a tower out of blocks, or designing as a storytelling playscape scene. Construction play promotes thinking, problem solving, and persistence in completing a task. Loose Parts such as small tree stumps, tree cookies, clay bricks, cardboard tubes, yarn spindles, and wooden spools spark the creativity of children with diverse abilities. This play supports them in developing spatial relationship concepts and mathematical thinking, and, most important, gives children with diverse abilities a sense of accomplishment. Because there is no right or wrong way to construct using Loose Parts, these materials empower children with diverse abilities to be innovative, flexible, determined, adaptable, and imaginative. Take four-year-old Max, who has been mourning the loss of his father to a car accident. He has entered into selective mutism and chooses not to talk or express his anguish. Every morning he comes into the educational ecosystem and goes straight to the construction space. He spends most of the time building towers and knocking them down. This goes on for months. His towers grow and become more complex, but he immediately knocks them down. To allow Max to process what is going on internally, the educators have created a separate construction space for other children. They want him to grieve and express what he is feeling. Finally, one day, he builds a tall tower and does not knock it down. He walks up to the educator and quietly says, "Can you write a sign that says, 'Max built this tower for Daddy'?" Max has continued to heal and little by little engages in play with other children. He has received the support of a therapist who comes into the classroom and works with the educators to support Max in his healing.

Provide a variety of Loose Parts that children with diverse abilities can use in designing, engineering, and constructing. Moving Loose Parts into different areas helps children explore varied possibilities. Rocks balance differently on a smooth surface than on grass, for example. Combining different Loose Parts increases interest and engagement. Cardboard tubes combined with wooden blocks challenge children to build with both flat and round surfaces.

Because they can represent most any object or being, gourds are a fabulous open-ended natural material to stimulate creativity and imagination. For children new to open-ended Loose Parts, provide concrete items such as dolls alongside the Loose Parts to support representational thinking (for example, "She picked a big pumpkin" or "Grandma is playing the guitar").

Children design, construct, and explore body movements with iridescent Mylar tubes. Lightweight cylindrical materials are wonderful for developing gross grasp strength, and children with low muscle tone or endurance can sustain play with lightweight materials for longer periods. Adjust the location to play at the tabletop and consider a lipped tray to contain items for children who use a wheelchair.

These mini wooden ladders (made for birds) build strength and bimanual coordination skills as children bend them to create make-believe lands or representational scenes with people of diverse ages and backgrounds.

A basket of matching colored beanbags and Velcro dots invites children to create their own games. The items are flexible in adapting to children's capacities; for example, children who need additional movement can use the dots for gross-motor activities such as hopscotch, while children who require less movement during play can design patterns with them.

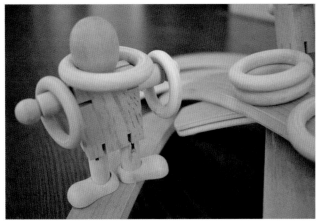

Children can design people with all different abilities by manipulating the wooden robots, creating wheelchairs with the blocks, or adding halos and braces with maple rings. The curved wooden arches and small circles invite critical thinking about how to carefully balance the items, a playful way to develop frustration tolerance.

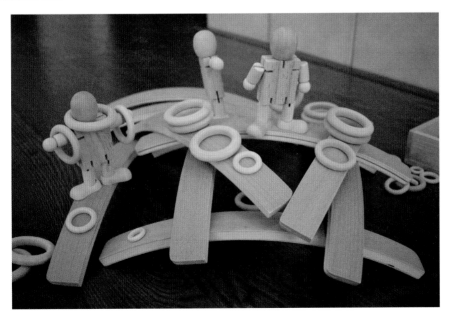

Chapter 7
Supporting the Whole Child

Inclusive environments are essential to support children and disrupt current ableist cultural beliefs in educational settings. Children with diverse abilities must never be defined only by their limitations or disability. To include every child, we must focus on the whole person. This idea of the whole child can be easily neglected when we focus on building mastery of an activity or a need to learn English. Inclusion is about building communities that encourage and celebrate children's achievements. Inclusion is also about building communities with other agencies and surrounding areas and groups to improve educational opportunities and conditions within their localities. The more people come together to support children, the more the entire community thrives.

The Division for Early Childhood Education of the Council for Exceptional Children (2014), an international organization, recommends that educators provide support and services in a natural and inclusive environment. Tony Booth, Mel Ainscow, and Denise Kingston (2006) introduced the *Index for Inclusion: Developing Play, Learning and Participation in Early Years and Childcare in the United Kingdom* and proposed that a collaboration involving educators, children, their families, and the wider community supports developmental outcomes. The index offers expectations and developmental outcomes that children can achieve. Each measure is supported with challenging questions that promote reflection. The reflection guides educators to evaluate their practices, then plan and implement new practices to promote sustainable change. The index recognizes three dimensions in developing inclusive educational ecosystems: creating inclusive cultures, producing inclusive policies, and evolving inclusive practices.

The key lesson from the *Index for Inclusion* is that it is guided by values, not standardized outcomes. Values are deep-seated beliefs that facilitate action. To create an inclusive ecosystem, we must define our values and ensure that they serve as the moral and ethical underpinnings of all our practices. Inclusion evolves when our values are visible in all practices and understood by everyone in the ecosystem. When educators clearly express their values and make them visible, they weave a moral argument in support of children with diverse abilities.

We must understand that inclusion is not attained solely by the child's placement in a certain educational setting. Instead, it is a daily practice and commitment to see children with diverse abilities as more than a label. Inclusive ecosystems must commit to working daily to dismantle prejudice and discrimination. This happens only when we establish and pursue common goals and values.

When we observe children, we learn that the developmental domains are connected and influence one another. Every part of the child works in concert to help them grow and develop. The same is true for children with diverse abilities. The Association for Supervision and Curriculum Development outlined an approach to whole-child education (ASCD 2012). The methodology includes five tenets based on child-development theory and recognizes that every child has the right to be healthy, safe, engaged, supported, and challenged. I would add that children also have the right to play and inhabit playful and joyful ecosystems. The educator creates those inclusive ecosystems where children's strengths guide their learning and development. When children experience a sense of belonging, they acquire the knowledge, skills, and dispositions to be successful in their own way. An inclusive and equitable environment focuses on promoting children's strengths while addressing their comprehensive needs through the shared responsibility of students, families, schools, and communities. The placement of children with diverse abilities must always be guided by the child's strengths and the family's sense of an environment that will afford their child the best opportunity to participate as a valued member of the community.

Therapeutic Opportunities in the Environment

Play is a fun, enjoyable activity that expands self-expression, self-knowledge, self-actualization, and self-efficacy. Play relieves feelings of stress and boredom, connects us to people in a positive way, stimulates creative thinking and exploration, regulates our emotions, and boosts our egos (Landreth 2012). Play gives children hope as they face difficult life challenges. This is why children with diverse abilities need to be fully engaged in play. Regrettably, play has been identified by many writers as children's work. As educators, we must let go of our need to classify or validate play as "work"; we just need to understand that for children play is crucial and the most important thing in their world. Children live in a world of the present. Many of the experiences they encounter in the adult world are future-oriented, abstract, and difficult to understand. Rather, we must allow children to be children without adding pressure to change and be ready for the next steps in their life. We must embrace the idea that childhood has intrinsic value by itself and not solely view it as preparation for kindergarten or adulthood. Play needs to be respected for its intrinsic value and not as a vehicle to teach adult expectations. This is particularly important for children with diverse abilities, as they already have many challenges to overcome daily. Play is intrinsically complete. Children do not require an external reward when they play. When educators create multiple opportunities to play, we help children learn to live in the world, exploring and experimenting and understanding the meanings, rules, symbols, and values in their own ways.

When children play, they are fully present physically, mentally, emotionally, and socially. Therapists find a world of information to observe and record as children use Loose Parts in an inclusive ecosystem. Loose Parts become a vehicle for expressing and conveying ideas and perhaps strong emotions. In play children share feelings that otherwise are too threatening to express, projecting their emotions as they bury stones in the sand, use a stick to shoot a dragon, or hide a baby doll in a blanket, representing a new sibling's arrival into the household. In an inclusive environment, therapy must be dynamic and follow the children's interests and ideas. Therapists can follow program requirements and policies and still select Loose Parts that develop relationships for and with children. These Loose Parts can be incorporated into the ecosystem for other children to use. The same is true for adaptive equipment. Fidgets, pop tubes, glitter wands, play eyeglasses, and adaptive silicone handles can be incorporated as Loose Parts for all children to explore. As I wrote this book, I worked closely with Rachel Marks, an occupational therapist. She offered suggestions and recommendations on how the Loose Parts that you see in the photo captions throughout the book would support children with diverse abilities. The more we create ecosystems that are inclusive and facilitate play, the more children with diverse abilities will be part of the community. For instance, Devon has asthma and needs a daily infusion of asthma medication through a nebulizer. The treatment takes time and requires Devon to sit while the nebulizer is in use. The educators carefully plan how to administer the infusion without distracting or bringing attention to Devon. Instead of saying, "Devon, time to use the nebulizer," they invite Devon and other children to join in Loose Parts play. An educator sits with the children and supervises the treatment while the children play. Devon gets his treatment without leaving the classroom or sitting by himself in an isolated area. Other times they invite Devon and other children to listen as an educator reads a book. The children in the classroom know that Devon needs treatment for his asthma. His family has come into the classroom, and Devon has explained to the children how he uses his nebulizer. He proudly responds to questions the children ask.

We need to follow a team approach to design and implement practices that best support children with diverse abilities. Educators, counselors, therapists, family members, school districts or external service providers, and, most important, the child must have a shared understanding of the strengths and challenges and set goals to move forward. Communication is crucial to ensure that therapeutic support happens within the context of children's play. Engaging an occupational or play therapist's support when selecting and adapting Loose Parts can be incredibly helpful. Meet frequently with the entire therapeutic team and families to plan new Loose Parts, tools, and materials to add to the ecosystem. Exploring and playing with the Loose Parts helps everyone analyze the items and find adaptations that will be helpful and engaging to children.

To create inclusive and equitable environments, we need to shift our view of children with diverse abilities. We need to discover their strengths and see them as capable and competent. We must not only find specific therapeutic strategies but delve deeper to build relationships and establish rapport. We must develop a profound and abiding belief in their capacities and resiliency to be constructively self-directing, and we must create opportunities for children to be the protagonists of their own knowledge. Children are quite capable of appropriately directing their own growth when they are granted freedom to play, discover, and build relationships that allow them to be their authentic selves and process feelings and experiences that are painful or hurtful. This is possible with children with diverse abilities and more generally with children who have experienced trauma in their lives. We must give equal status to children with diverse abilities, acknowledging their individual and group identities by naming their disabilities and valuing their difference while finding commonalities. Invisibility only denies children's identities and promotes disconnection and isolation.

Our role as educators is to walk with children and not always lead. Standing side by side, listening, observing, and being present gives way for children's inner capacities to emerge. When children know they can trust you and relax in your presence, they can reach their full potential in their own time, through their own processes and abilities. When a child is supported to be their authentic self and their stories are received with compassion, empathy, and care, they thrive and can begin to process their emotions and feelings in safety.

Building Relationships with Families

If we are to facilitate an ecosystem that allows children to be their authentic selves, we must be vulnerable and open to changing our perspectives. As early childhood educators, we have a responsibility to create conditions so families feel respected, welcomed, and valued. We must be sensitive to the complex and ever-changing roles families play in their children's lives and see ourselves as co-facilitators and co-learners with the children and families. With warmth, interest, care, understanding, genuineness, and empathy, we can make sustainable change. When we assume this respectful approach as co-learners with children and families, we more effectively navigate cross-cultural barriers. Families and children learn that we are humbly ready to learn from them and with them, and they gain the power to make decisions and become an authentic part of a supportive team.

Getting to know the families helps us genuinely strengthen our relationships. Families help us understand what is going on in children's lives outside the classroom. They provide clues to understanding the meaning of a child's play. When families share a story of growth they noticed at home, together we can continue to support that growth. When I worked with children with diverse abilities and visited their homes, the families' enthusiasm in discovering a simple milestone helped me notice new things. For instance, Erin, an eighteen-month-old who had limited vision, learned how to pick up a bead from a bowl and transfer it into a second bowl. Together with the family, we planned what to do next that would support her development.

When my youngest daughter was in preschool, we had a season with very heavy rain, and one day our house flooded. As the house was flooding, my daughter came down the stairs holding an umbrella and wearing her yellow raincoat and rain boots. In the moment, I just thought it was "cute." Days later, her behavior changed, and she started testing limits. We could not figure out what was happening. Luckily the talented educators at Children's Circle Nursery School pointed out to me that my daughter was afraid of having another flood in our house. Thankfully, I trusted the educators because we had built a strong relationship that exists even today. I knew they had my family's best interests at heart, and their compassion and gentle guidance helped me restore a feeling of safety for my daughter.

When early childhood educational ecosystems become a community and families get to know one another, the level of support increases. Families who lack a strong support system or who live far away from close relatives can find friendships and develop strong bonds with one another. With these relationships, children thrive and everyone's acceptance of differences grows. When families make communal connections, they feel better about themselves, have less anxiety, and learn to ask for help and support as needed. Families who participate in the community are better adjusted and more likely to respond to their children in positive and enhancing ways. Creating spaces where families gather as they drop off their children supports the building of community. Form a courtyard with Loose Parts where children play as families sit or stand around to talk, or create a place where a family member can play with their child to help them transition into the day. An area where two or three children and their families can play until the children feel ready to join the other children is not only responsive to the child's needs but also reassures the family that they are welcome in the ecosystem. The more opportunities we take to develop community, the easier our work will be, and the more we accomplish collaborative goals, the more the children will benefit. In a tight community, a sense of social justice emerges and a protective circle forms around the children as families come together to support one another. Children learn to respect one another and to embrace differences even as they find commonalities.

Anti-Ableist Education

Children and adults interact in early childhood ecosystems through a wide range of intersecting individual and group identities, including gender, race, ability, socioeconomic status, ethnicity, culture, and others. Contrary to popular beliefs, young children notice differences, and they make choices based on their previous understandings and experiences. They categorize and evaluate people by race, gender, and physical characteristics. Children can understand that social hierarchies are determined by systems of power and oppression, which are internalized through societal messages promoting stereotypical images and messages about people—and particularly children with diverse abilities. To disrupt negative representation and eliminate the stigma that children with diverse abilities feel in educational systems, we must create ecosystems where children are valued and included with respect and authenticity and where they interact with one another regardless of their diverse abilities, race, ethnicity, gender, socioeconomics, or culture. As educators, we must address ableism, the persistent devaluing of children with diverse abilities and the belief that a disability is an inherently diminished state of being (Campbell 2009). We need to embrace inclusive language and help children develop the language to communicate and depose the negative discourse that sometimes surrounds children with diverse abilities.

Anti-ableist education can help undo the damage caused by ableist discourse and practices. Louise Derman-Sparks and Julie Olsen Edwards (2020) have presented the early childhood profession with a framework to guide us in providing anti-bias education for all children. The following four goals of anti-bias education help early childhood educators support young children in exploring issues of bias and discrimination across all aspects of diversity to promote inclusivity.

Goal 1: Each child will demonstrate self-awareness, confidence, family pride, and positive social identities.

As families arrive, have children explore their names in different languages, including braille and American Sign Language. Morning gatherings can serve as a forum to create community. Having conversations about who we are as a group and talking about our family members and our culture supports inclusion. Introduce songs in various languages and invite families to share their favorite childhood songs. Include communication modalities that represent the diversity of students in the classroom, such as cards with sign language, braille books and blocks, and sets of visual communication cards or sticks. Use word game letter tiles in braille as a Loose Part. Read books that show diversity with respect and pride, representing children in active roles and as active members of the community and including diverse family structures, ethnicities, disabilities, gender identities, and cultures. Including images of children with diverse abilities in active roles can help disrupt the stereotypes and biases that show children with diverse abilities being disengaged or incapable. Print photos of children and glue them into tubes or wooden blocks to use in the construction zone or for storytelling. Place adaptive equipment and materials around the classroom for all children to explore. For instance, at Lincoln Community Preschool, children use fidgets around the room in dramatic play, for testing their strength, and in the construction space. When fidgets are provided as Loose Parts, children with diverse abilities can use them to help self-regulate without being the only ones in the classroom using them.

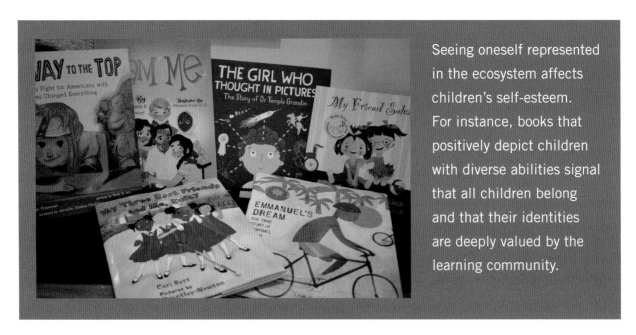

Seeing oneself represented in the ecosystem affects children's self-esteem. For instance, books that positively depict children with diverse abilities signal that all children belong and that their identities are deeply valued by the learning community.

Goal 2: Each child will experience comfort and joy with human diversity, have accurate language for human differences, and form deep, caring human connections.

We want every child to have confidence and feel pride in their competence and abilities. It is essential to provide opportunities for children to understand their abilities and how these abilities are similar to and different from others. Because children control how they use Loose Parts, they can better explore their capacities. Loose Parts play facilitates conversations among children who can see that every child may use the tools, objects, and materials differently and that they all have various capacities, abilities, and ideas that can be shared fairly, regardless of their abilities. As children learn to respect and appreciate one another's abilities and capacities, they become more willing to challenge stereotypes and name-calling. They share ideas about accessibility to promote interactions and collaboration, strengthening their ability to advocate for one another. When children play together without an adult dictating, for example, that we must help our friend in the wheelchair, we are building ecosystems where children learn to navigate new situations and feel comfortable discussing differences in identities.

Young children are curious and full of questions. When they notice another child with a diverse ability, their first instinct is to ask about it. Offer a short but matter-of-fact description to answer the question. It is crucial that the response is factual and does not carry any loaded agenda to make the child with diverse abilities feel shame. For example, suppose a new child uses a wheelchair. The educator introduces the child with a simple comment, "Children, I want you to meet Alexandra. She will be joining our class. As you can see, Alexandra uses a wheelchair. Some people's muscles work a little differently, and her wheelchair helps her move around, just like your legs help you. Alexandra, do you want to share the book you brought from home?" Using a positive explanation rather than referring to differences from a deficit perspective gives children the language and context to feel comfortable around differences. For instance, Cecilia and Joshua are working on an art piece using bottle caps. As Joshua starts to put the bottle caps around the frame, Cecilia says, "No, Joshua, put them inside." Joshua continues to line the bottle caps outside the perimeter of the frame. In a louder voice, Cecilia says, "No, they go here." Educator Claudia comes over and says, "Cecilia, let's use sign language to tell Joshua what you want." She helps Cecilia communicate that she wants Joshua to place the bottle caps inside the frame. Joshua nods and puts the bottle caps inside the frame. Cecilia and Joshua continue to work on their piece of artwork together. Educator Claudia notices that they have started using simple sign language to communicate. The next day, when Mauricio wants Joshua to move the tree stumps into the storytelling playscape, Cecilia comes over and says to Mauricio, "Joshua uses his hands to talk; let me show you," while demonstrating how to say hello in sign language.

As you listen to children's questions, ask some questions of your own to better understand their perceptions. For example, "When you say you do not want to play with Alona because she is different, what does different mean to you? Do you have anything that you both like to do?" Discussing abilities and diversity leads to acceptance and respect.

Goal 3: Each child will increasingly recognize unfairness, have language to describe unfairness, and understand that unfairness hurts.

It is not uncommon that power dynamics emerge in early childhood ecosystems. Children test their power in multiple ways, like when they climb high, construct tall block towers, and engage in dramatic or symbolic play with other children. For example: Charlotte and Eliana are designing a building using Mylar-covered cardboard tubes. Thomas wants to join, but the girls decide that he is too slow and would not finish building the tower. Thomas quietly leaves and finds a book to read. Educator Harry listened to what happened and walked over to Thomas. He sits down and puts his arm around Thomas. Harry quietly says, "That probably did not feel so good. I know I would not like it if other people told me I can't play with them." During the afternoon group gathering, Harry uses puppets to introduce a scenario in which one puppet did not want to play with the other puppet because it looked different. Benjamin, another child, says, "That is not fair; we need to play together." Harry takes this opportunity to ask questions about fairness. "Is this fair that we don't play with other children because they don't do the things the way we do? Is this right? Does this hurt anyone? What else could we do to make this moment just? Why do people feel like this?" The children have many ideas about what is fair, and they ask one another questions. Harry knows that this is just one day in the journey to disrupt ableism. However, he also knows that children are incredibly competent and capable of understanding that people can be different and yet play with one another. It is crucial that educators focus on fairness and not equality (everyone treated the same). There will always be times when children need extra support and help. This can be explained to children with a simple example, "If one child is hurt and needs a Band-Aid, would it be helpful to give all the children in the classroom a Band-Aid?" When there is trust and a strong sense of belonging, children better understand fairness and act accordingly.

Goal 4: Each child will demonstrate empowerment and the skills to act, with others or alone, against prejudice and/or discriminatory actions.

Rocio and Manuel are using tubes, colorful bandages, and other plastic connectors to create a machine to help Saul, a classmate, feel better. Saul is in the hospital with pneumonia. As other children notice what Rocio and Manuel are doing, they share ideas and make different breathing machine prototypes. As the day progresses, the children continue to work together and discuss how it is not fair that Saul has to be in the hospital and cannot play with them. The conversation continues during group gatherings, so the educators talk about how sometimes unfairness happens, but they can help one another and help Saul feel loved as he remains in the hospital. They work together to create a box with Saul's favorite

Loose Parts that educators can bring to the hospital when they visit Saul. Even though this chapter is not solely focused on Loose Parts, we hope it introduces the importance of creating equitable and inclusive ecosystems where children with diverse abilities thrive. We invite educators committed to equity and social justice to reimagine early childhood ecosystems and communities where everyone is valued and feels safe to engage in meaningful conversations about human differences. Young children are more than capable of considering the nature of oppression, and they need to be provided with tools to recognize and resist ableism. It is only then that we will have sustainable change.

silicone fidgets

squish balls

Sensory items like silicone fidgets, squish balls, chewy necklaces, silicone scrubbers, handmade crochet sponges, and adaptive items like silicone grip cuffs, foam tubing, protective headphones, loop scissors, and easy-grip markers and crayons enable children to participate in daily activities. Zoom balls provide a bilateral coordination and motor-planning challenge that strengthens collaboration among children as they work together to slide the ball back and forth.

chewy necklaces

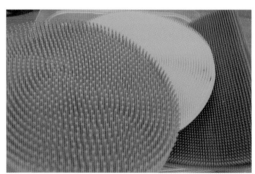

silicone scrubbers

hand-made crochet sponges

foam tubing

silicone grip cuffs

protective
headphones

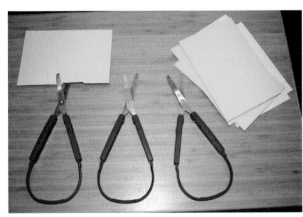

loop scissors

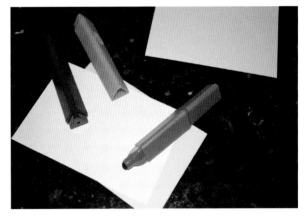

easy grip markers and crayons

zoom balls

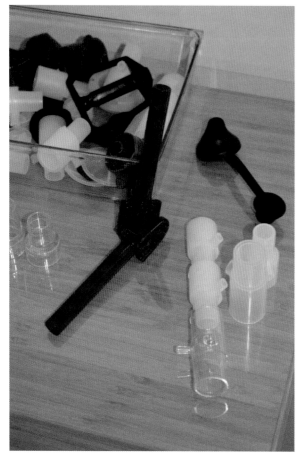

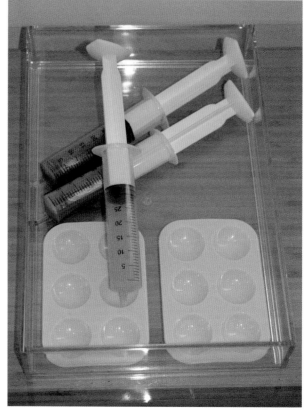

Provide easily sanitized Loose Parts for children needing short- or long-term stays in the hospital. Exploring typical hospital items on their own terms may help ease children's anxiety regarding medical procedures. Incorporating items that a child may see their doctors using into engaging activities can help children process their experiences in the hospital or health care setting. They can explore color mixing and manipulating the syringe themselves to become more comfortable with the tool. Smaller syringes or pipettes work well for younger children or those developing fine-motor strength and dexterity.

Add mini Jenga pieces to the quiet space for children to play with during one-on-one work with a therapist or to occupy them as they receive an infusion asthma treatment.

Children can play together or alongside one another, clicking or banging metal caps. Have headphones available to prevent dysregulation from noise overstimulation.

Chapter 8
Acknowledging Funds
of Knowledge

Our ultimate goal as
culturally responsive
teachers is to help de-
pendent learners learn
how to learn. We want
them to have the abil-
ity to size up any task,
map out a strategy for
completing it, and then
execute the plan. That's
what independent
learners do.
—Zaretta Hammond

Often educators deny the fact that our work is political. The reality is that to advocate for children, we *must* be political and fully informed as to what influences our
work. Without this understanding, we will fail children and families.

Our work begins with understanding that children with diverse abilities and
families have powerful funds of knowledge that they bring with them as they
become part of the early childhood ecosystem. In 1992 Carlos G. Vélez-Ibáñez and
James B. Greenberg introduced the concept of funds of knowledge. They recognized that the historical accumulation of families' abilities, knowledge, assets, and
cultural ways of being were left out of the educational systems. Norma González,
Luis C. Moll, and Cathy Amanti (2005) expanded the work and explained ways to
recognize children and families' funds of knowledge and integrate them into educational systems. Children's and families' funds of knowledge can be identified as

- intellectual and personal background knowledge,
- accumulated life experiences,
- skills and knowledge used to navigate everyday social contexts, and
- worldviews structured by broader historically and politically influenced social
  forces.

Engaging Families' Funds of Knowledge

Throughout the book, we have integrated the funds of knowledge and diverse
perspectives from families, colleagues, researchers, and theorists. When we educate and care for children with diverse abilities, it is essential to do so with a profound understanding of the collective funds of knowledge.

In this chapter, we invite you to use the specific lens that will help you identify the funds of knowledge in your educational ecosystems. Who are the children, families, and colleagues that share the ecosystem? What stories do they tell?
What are the funds of knowledge shared by the larger community ecosystem,
and how do you integrate them into your practices? Family support is essential

for continuity and stability, especially because children with diverse abilities are highly vulnerable to changes in routine. Educators can serve as a sounding board to help families find that stability. Unfortunately, some families tell a different story. They tell about times when the educator took the stance of an expert and would not listen to the strategies and experiences the families shared. In the most extreme cases, the children were kicked out of the program. As difficult as it is to listen to these stories, I think they provide those of us in the early childhood profession a thought-provoking base to question and reflect on our practices.

In almost all the conversations I have with families of children with diverse abilities, they tell me of their struggles to get the necessary resources to support their child. They share their grief for the lost dream of having the "perfect" child. I hear stories of joy as their child with diverse abilities achieves a new goal or meets a new milestone. I have learned that all parents do their best to love and care for their child, and with the proper support, they become a champion advocate for them. I also have learned that as humans, we all have emotions and we are imperfect. Without emotions we wouldn't be capable of intimacy and healthy relationships. It is through this imperfection that we make powerful connections with other humans.

Understanding and drawing on funds of knowledge serve as a stepping-stone to selecting, curating, and infusing Loose Parts that further support children with diverse abilities. For example, when Ruby joins the classroom community, she begins to share her interest in gardening in various ways. Ruby's speech is limited, and she often prefers to play alone. She makes flowers using bottle caps and transfers her designs into drawings. Outdoors Ruby lines up empty containers and cans around the perimeter of the yard, then cuts leaves and plants to put in each receptacle. Her work goes on for days. As the educators observe and record Ruby's interests, ideas, and skills, they become curious about Ruby's outside experiences with plants and flowers. The educators invite her family to share stories. The family is hesitant at first. They share their concerns and what they have heard from others about the challenges Ruby will have in her schooling. To their surprise, they soon realize that the educators are more interested in what Ruby knows and how they can support her interests. During the conversation, the educators learn that Ruby spends time with her family gardening and growing vegetables. Ruby's mother loves flowers, and they are a staple in their home's decor. Ruby helps sort seeds for gardening. The family lives together on a small farm owned by her grandparents. Ruby's grandparents had worked as migrant farmers in California, where they learned to grow a variety of fruits and vegetables. When they had saved enough money to buy their own home, they knew that they would plant a garden to feed the family.

The educators share their documentation with the speech therapist, who is excited to integrate Ruby's interests into her therapy. They invite Ruby's grandparents to start a garden in the play yard. Ruby's dad helps build raised garden beds. He invites the class to create a plan for which vegetables will go in which container. The children join Ruby as she shows them how to sort seeds. Molly, the speech therapist, uses these moments to introduce new vocabulary to help Ruby while supporting all the children's language development. The children sort the seed envelopes into piles and create labels to add to the garden. In this simple yet effective act, Ruby's family, the educators, and the therapist use existing funds of knowledge to support children in acquiring math, literacy, social justice, and collaboration skills. Ruby and her family become valued members of the community. Soon the family invites the children to visit Ruby's house, where they make a special meal using the farm's harvest, which the children help gather.

The children collect acorns, pebbles, and pine cones from the trees that border the farm's perimeter, sorting and trading the natural Loose Parts. They negotiate and argue, with Ruby right in the middle of the negotiations as she is becoming a participating member of the community. Little by little, Ruby increases her ability to communicate verbally, and her interest in using other languages to express her thinking grows stronger. The children notice that Ruby has begun playing with them, and they invite her to join more frequently. The children in the program learned to respect and value the funds of knowledge Ruby shares.

This story demonstrates how funds of knowledge and strong collaborations are invaluable in supporting children with diverse abilities. It shows us how putting the child at the center can change interactions and the entire community's outcome. Engaging families can be as simple as inviting them to help you collect Loose Parts for the program or listening to unexpected discoveries that happened at home or on weekend adventures. When listening to families who have children with diverse abilities, you will soon learn how incredibly creative they are. They will go out of their way to find ordinary objects that engage children's interests. Ask families what the children play with at home and what ordinary objects they use: lids and plastic storage containers, buttons, napkin rings, chenille stems, metal rings from canning jars, washers and extra nuts and bolts, metal tubes from plumbing projects, and endless other ideas.

Providing ways for families to contribute facilitates a sense of community. To invite families to help you collect Loose Parts, place baskets at the entrance, including photographs of any Loose Parts you are particularly looking for. You will be surprised at how eager families are to help you, and they will bring you Loose Parts that you have not even considered. One of my favorite unexpected discoveries was dry okra pods. Children made intricate designs as they combined them with other natural items. Set a table with Loose Parts where families can sit and play with the children in the program. Designate adults-only play nights where family members can play together. I have fond memories of the play nights at my daughter's nursery school. We played with blocks, created sculptures with clay, and used tempera paint to make works of art. We left a note for the children to see the next day. As adults, it was fun to have the opportunity just to play. Families of children with diverse abilities often feel isolated and stressed. Life challenges, frequent change, and anxiety confront them continually. It is not enough to send a motivational message or to tell them that things will work out; they need more. In these moments of stress, we can turn to what children have known for centuries: the power of play. Children play without an adult telling them what to do. They find a sense of flow and get lost in imaginary worlds. What is even more critical is that play brings laughter, relaxation, and understanding beyond any motivational message. Creating moments for families to play with Loose Parts together goes a long way in building community and helping families find support.

When possible, make home visits. Most families are open and honored to have educators visit. Listening and asking questions will help you learn from the family. Visits also help the family feel included and valued. Prepare a bag with Loose Parts to give to the families and include a handout in families' home language about how the Loose Parts support children's learning, stimulate creativity, and engage the brain. Understanding the value of Loose Parts reassures families that their children are learning. Play brings families together and reminds children of the unconditional love that surrounds them. Unconditional love may not be the reality for some families, but play can open the door to connectedness. Focus on the joy of spending extra time together. The Loose Parts bag also serves as an invitation for families to look for ordinary objects they can use with their children. Many of the Loose Parts invitations and provocations in this book can be easily re-created at home. Loose Parts are also less expensive than many commercial toys, making them easier for families to incorporate into everyday play activities.

Invite families into your classroom to share their talents and expertise, if necessary reassuring them that the children are eager to learn from them. Whatever their interest, it is always welcome. The essential purpose is showing children that their families are valued and that educators recognize how proud children are of family members' knowledge. Be creative and find ways to include families that can't physically come into the classroom. They can tape a story for you to listen to during group gatherings or send a video showing how they make the family's favorite food. With today's technology, we can find ways to include all families.

Engaging Children's Funds of Knowledge

Children teach us powerful lessons. When we listen, observe, and notice what they do and share, we learn that they are capable, creative, and filled with knowledge and ideas. For example, Theo often gets overwhelmed when play becomes too active. He finds the imagination fabric (large gauze fabric that is big enough to build forts and transparent enough to see the children) and encloses himself to avoid the activity. He knows when he needs to separate himself and has found a way to self-protect. Often, as adults, we fail to recognize our own emotions until they manifest abruptly. Theo's skills and strategies are something adults can replicate, maybe not physically hiding under the fabric, but finding a place to take a moment away.

Using the concept of funds of knowledge as a lens or a theoretical framework helps educators analyze and better understand societal and cultural influences on how children make meaning of the world. We must continually remind ourselves that knowledge is not an individualized internal process; instead, learning is co-constructed through children's participation in social and cultural practices and interactions with family and community. Children's experiences affect the way they make meaning in their play. Furthermore, researchers argue that children's access to funds of knowledge and experiences from their families and communities may influence the distribution of power, agency, and choice within classroom peer cultures (González, Moll, and Amanti 2005).

Children's funds of knowledge are clearly seen in sociodramatic play. For instance, Valentina plays at the mud table, adding dirt and water to a tall pot. She stirs and adds white pebbles, then walks over to the grass area and picks some grass and leaves from a nearby bush. She returns to the kitchen and uses a ladle to pour the mixture into a bowl. She adds the grass and leaves on top of the mix. She picks up a spoon and pretends to taste what she just cooked. She exclaims, "Me gusta el pozole" (I like pozole). Pozole is a traditional Mexican soup made with hominy and served with fresh lettuce or cabbage. Valentina is learning to speak English and is starting to translate some words. Her family is concerned she may be exhibiting some signs of speech delay. The educators have intentionally infused Loose Parts to encourage Valentina to continue to express her cultural funds of knowledge. They are confident that using the familiar Loose Parts and authentic tools will support language acquisition. For example, educators provide a mortar and pestle for Vivian to grind familiar spices. When Vivian grinds a cinnamon stick, she describes how it tastes when her grandmother adds it to hot chocolate, as a tradition passes from generation to generation. A culturally relevant, inclusive, and reflective curriculum focuses on the authentic values of culture and not just the surface manifestations such as artifacts, multicultural food fairs, and celebrations of secular holidays. Instead, there is an intentional focus on the history, beliefs, values, traditions, and language, which help define culture holistically and use children's and families' funds of knowledge.

Another example of how children's funds of knowledge contribute is seen as Caleb lines up small tubes and counts them, "1, 2, 3, 4, 5, 6, 7, 8, 9, like Hanukkah." He had just celebrated the Festival of Lights with his family. Lamar, who is close by and carefully listening, comes over to Caleb, takes more tubes, lines them up, and says, "Home." He is letting Caleb know that in his house, they celebrate Kwanzaa. Both children bring their cultural funds of knowledge into their play. They support each other, and they learn about each other's family life and culture. This simple exchange shows how children learn to respect different perspectives when they play together and co-construct knowledge about each other's way of being in the world. This skill allows children to value the contributions of their peers with diverse abilities.

Funds of Knowledge from Advisory Members

A community's power is that profound sense of knowing you are not alone as you work to achieve your goals. In writing this book, I drew on the funds of knowledge of friends, families, and expert colleagues. I hope I have illustrated the importance of forming collaborations when creating accommodations and using Loose Parts at home and in early childhood education ecosystems. As I began this book, I knew that my experience in caring for and educating children with diverse abilities had to be expended with the funds of knowledge from families, experts, and the children themselves. Michelle Grant-Groves, founder of the i3 Institute and the Center of Gravity Lab School in Pleasant Hill, California, gracefully agreed to reach out and guide a group of colleagues in a powerful conversation. She used a Design in Mind (DIM) hive-mind protocol to build many ideas as a way to engage the advisory committee members in a collective decision-making process. This protocol is included in our cowritten book, *Design in Mind: A Framework for Sparking Ideas, Collaboration, and Innovation in Early Education.* With that desire and idea in mind, I reached out to friends and colleagues and formed an advisory council to help me solve "sticky points," exchange ideas, provide accommodations, and find innovative research to support this writing.

The diverse advisory members not only spoke on behalf of children but also reminded me to acknowledge how the historical and political climates have influenced our perspectives and views of children. In this part of the book, I hope you will see how each advisory member's knowledge, experience, and ideas help make this book robust. Their recommendations and advice helped me stay grounded and continuously reminded me to focus on seeing the children's capabilities and competencies, not just their disabilities. The following are some of the recommendations collectively shared by advisory members. I do hope that I have captured both the group and individual wisdom.

Remember to focus on the whole child and not just assessment or IEP goals. We must open our minds to understand how children perceive the world. Wonder with children and co-construct knowledge with them. Children are more than just what adults want them to be. They have their own important ways of being in the world. Consider how you can share power with children rather than have power over them.

As you plan to create inclusive and culturally responsive environments, ensure that every child is represented in an authentic and respectful way. The focus must be on children's individual strengths as well as the strengths of the combined ecosystem. Concentrate on Loose Parts that tell the stories of the families in the program, but be sure to include imagery that represents cultures not present in the community too. Create protocols that are centered on supporting the whole child and increase educators' knowledge about the children's way of being in the world. For example, plan home visits and family gatherings throughout the year where you get to know the children and family members. Photos of the children engaged in play with their families give children the opportunity to communicate and explore family diversity. Cultural responsiveness and inclusion require intentionality and constant engagement with children and families. Families come in multiple constellations that must be honored and respected. The more the ecosystem offers a sense of belonging for children with diverse abilities, the more their disability is normalized.

The advisory members reminded me that less is more and to find balance in the amount and types of Loose Parts infused into the ecosystem. When we include the materials and purposefully design early childhood ecosystems, children own the space and their creativity emerges. The materials and the environment are in real partnership with children, and they have a shared purpose. Allow children the time and space to explore their imaginations. Focus on the balance between spaces that allow children to play quietly and spaces that engage them in collaborative work. Organize the Loose Parts for easy reach and accessibility—organization is key to helping children get centered. As you come to know the children and their families, experiment and make changes to the environment so you are designing from knowledge and not from assumptions. Notice when there is developmental growth and respond to new interests or where children feel overstimulated.

Be aware of how materials might trigger an existing trauma. Children who have experienced deep trauma may not have the language to express their feelings. Be mindful in your response and know that the child may exhibit mistaken behaviors due to dysregulation. It is crucial that educators slow down and respond rather than react to the behavior. Guiding children softly can help them self-regulate and overcome the trauma.

As you plan the ecosystem for the first days of school, consider what an outsider will feel as they walk into the space. Consider how you can make your environment embrace flexibility, accessibility, and choices for children more organically. Aesthetics are important, and children with diverse abilities deserve to be surrounded by beautiful things. Lighting, colors, and natural materials enhance the way an environment looks. Incorporating works of art created by the children and community artists adds to the aesthetic qualities of the environment. Establish a process to display children's art in a way that is inclusive and not visually overwhelming, such as a wall dedicated to displaying the art. Rather than taping the artwork or pinning it into a bulletin board, consider using frames to honor children's work.

Offer children different entry points to engage in play. Consider physical, social, and emotional entry points. Children may enter play through storytelling, which can become an energizing activity. Think of materials that transform and invite children to design. Pair novelty with familiarity to allow children to reset and enter the circularity of the creative flow. Be flexible with the environment and let the children (not the curriculum or assessment tools) make decisions. Be bold and do not focus on meeting standards. Instead, add complexity because you see the children and understand their thinking. Ask yourself: What can I modify? What other Loose Parts can I add? For example, textures can either soothe or stimulate children. Keep a journal and record what you notice. Gather with colleagues, families, and the children and create a plan for making changes. Give up control and instead be open to transformation and the sharing of ideas and surprises. Revisit your own creative flow. In his 2009 book, *Drive*, Daniel Pink proposes the idea of supporting people to become intrinsically motivated—that is, using internal drives as a source of motivation. The same concept can be applied to children. Supporting children's internal drives and motivation will lead to greater understanding and relationship building.

Assistive technology becomes positive for children with diverse abilities when it is used to support play. Something as simple as adding longer handles goes a long way. Use digital technology to record stories that emerge as children play with Loose Parts. Highlighting what they are capable of and recording simple milestones can encourage and motivate children with diverse abilities. Integrating technological solutions can accommodate children with physical, sensory, or cognitive challenges and boost children's engagement.

Celebrations and gatherings create a sense of community. When families gather to share stories and exchange ideas, they find not only comfort but also a group of friends who can relate to their life challenges. They create a network where every child is cared for and supported and where families find the power and freedom to be themselves. You can let families know that you appreciate them and their dedication to their children. When you validate their strengths and abilities, you help build the skills they need to support their children.

When all funds of knowledge come together, a sense of community forms. Listening and including different perspectives and cultural voices promotes community inclusion and creates a sense of powerful freedom. Children with diverse abilities learn to participate in community events, activities, and gatherings and receive the support they need to be successful.

Key Reflections

- How might you gather the funds of knowledge of children and families in your classroom or program?
- What similarities did you notice among the funds of knowledge shared by the families in your program? What differences did you notice?
- What funds of knowledge do families of children with diverse abilities bring to the program?
- What are some ways you might apply the funds of knowledge of children and families to inform culturally relevant and inclusive programming (such as approaches to play, playful interactions, and inclusion)?
- How will you create inclusive and culturally sustainable gatherings and celebrations in your program?

Ask parents or community members with special skills or connections to gather unique Loose Parts. For instance, an installer may have extra carpet, tile, flooring, or other interestingly colored samples that can promote increased visual discrimination skills and provide new sensory experiences.

Children explore inserting schema by using Loose Parts and other tools and materials. Spheres of different sizes make the provocation more accessible and enhance independence for children with a decreased range of motion. Going on a walk to collect leaves keeps children connected to their community, increasing their funds of knowledge and promoting family engagement.

Wrapping yarn and rope on spindles is an inviting bonding activity that children can do at home with family members. It helps develop bilateral coordination. Using one hand for stability while the other does the main action is necessary for daily functions such as dressing.

Advisory Facilitator

Starting in 1996, Michelle Grant-Groves has been a teacher, site administrator, systems administrator, coach, and coaching coordinator. Previous roles include 0–8 coordinating officer at Oakland Unified School District and equity and instructional program coordinator at San Francisco Unified School District Early Education Department. Michelle holds a BA in child development, research, and policy from San Francisco State University and a master's degree in P–3 early education from Mills College, including postgraduate research in P–3 alignment assessments and evaluations.

Advisory Members

Tatiana Borda earned her master's degree in early childhood education and special education credential at Mills College. Her teaching is based on an inquiry-based, constructivist model. Social and emotional development is at the core of her teaching philosophy, along with providing an anti-bias curriculum. Tatiana's strong background in special education helps her identify and serve the needs and learning abilities of all children, including developing linguistically, culturally, and developmentally appropriate IFSP and IEP goals that support each child's individual needs.

Jane Cawley is an early childhood and adult educator with fifty years of experience working with children, families, and educators. After retiring as executive director of Nova Scotia College of Early Childhood Education (NSCECE), Jane joined the Physical Literacy in the Early Years (PLEY) research project at Dalhousie University. She is part-time faculty at Mount Saint Vincent University and NSCECE and has served as an educational consultant for Nova Scotia Early Childhood Development Intervention Services.

Kay Cutler is a professor of early childhood education at South Dakota State University, teaching early childhood methods and special education courses. She also directs the Fishback Center for Early Childhood Education. Her research focuses on critical thinking through visual thinking strategies (VTS) and on interdisciplinary design thinking with the work of the Rich Normality Design Collaborative.

Dr. Katheryn Ingrum has been in the field of early childhood education for over thirty years in a variety of positions. She has directed child care centers across the United States, including centers at the National Security Agency, the IRS, and the Pentagon. Katheryn Ingrum has taught a wide range of child development, family studies, and education courses at San Diego State University, UC San Diego, Grossmont College, and Citrus College. Dr. Ingrum was awarded the Barbara Chernofsky Lifetime Achievement Award in 2012 by San Diego County Child Care and Development Planning Council.

Kasey Kile has devoted her career to advocating for high-quality care for young children. She brings a wealth of knowledge from a constructivist approach through her more than fifteen years as a center director, training specialist, and adjunct instructor. As the director of professional development for Kodo Kids, Kasey works with educators and the engineering team to develop customized learning kits for programs.

Rachel Marks is an occupational therapist and graduate of San Jose State University's master of science in occupational therapy program. She studied human development and psychology with an emphasis on early childhood development and education at Sonoma State University. Throughout her career, she has enjoyed working directly with children and adults of many abilities and their families in school, home, and community settings. She feels especially rewarded when able to facilitate independence and participation in children's necessary and valued occupations—particularly play!

Debbie McMannis (right) has over thirty years of experience ranging from hands-on classroom teaching to statewide policy and decision-making as the former director of

the early education and support division of the California Department of Education. She served in the US Navy during Desert Storm. Debbie co-owns Lincoln Community Preschool as the toddler teacher and principal.

Casey Johnson (left) has over ten years of experience in early childhood education. Casey received her master's degree in human development from Pacific Oaks College. As a preschool-aged child, Casey herself was immersed in play education with Bev Bos, an internationally known and respected early childhood educator. Casey is formally trained in Resources for Infant Educarers (RIE) Foundations. She co-owns Lincoln Community Preschool alongside her mom, Debbie McMannis, and works as the preschool teacher and director.

Margie Perez-Sesser has been an early childhood educator since 1973, working as director of Head Start and Migrant Head Start, and as State Preschool WestEd consultant and Program for Infant Toddler Care (PITC) trainer. She was a full-time faculty member at Modesto Junior College and Cuesta College. She supervised the First-Step Perinatal Program in a drug and alcohol treatment program serving at-risk infants who were prenatally substance exposed. Margie has a bachelor's degree in Child Development from California State University, Stanislaus, and a master's degree in human development with a specialization in leadership in education and human services from Pacific Oaks College.

Clover Porche is a licensed clinical social worker. She works for UC San Francisco Benioff's Children's Hospital–Oakland as a psychotherapist, providing mental health services primarily to preschool-age children and their families. Clover graduated from San Francisco State with an undergraduate degree in child and adolescent development and a minor in child psychology, then obtained a graduate degree from the school of social work.

Diane Spahn is an eternal optimist (except in the morning before coffee), humorist, and advocate of children and educators. As an ECE educator for more than twenty-five years, she brings a constructivist approach to her role as the director of education for Kodo Kids. Spahn partners with Kodo's design, education, and engineering team and professional educators worldwide to develop intriguing products, training courses, public-speaking events, and customized kits of learning tools. Spahn is known among her colleagues for creating beautiful and enlivening materials and spaces for play and learning.

LaWanda Wesley serves as Oakland Unified School District's director of quality enhancement and professional development of early education. Dr. Wesley also codirected the California Consortium for Equity in Early Childhood Education Fellowship, a statewide leadership fellowship, and is the cofounder and codirector for the Center for Equity in Early Childhood Education in service of disrupting race inequities at the root cause. Wesley is coauthor of *Culturally Responsive Self-Care Practices for Early Childhood Educators* and *Trauma-Responsive Practices for Early Childhood Leaders: Creating and Sustaining Healing Engaged Organizations*.

Micayla Whitmer is a scholar of Deaf studies, disability studies, and critical race theory. Her research focuses primarily on the Deaf community, the Black Deaf community, and Black American Sign Language. She has worked as both an interpreter and educator in child care settings, witnessing the importance of having accessible language, accessible spaces, and accessible learning tools for all children.

Checklist of Considerations for Loose Parts for Children with Diverse Abilities

This checklist is designed to guide the process of designing Loose Parts to foster an inclusive and equitable early childhood ecosystem. The checklist provides ideas of the accommodations that can be made to Loose Parts to increase accessibility and engagement.

1. Sensory Development and Regulation

☐ Incorporate Loose Parts that promote sensory efficiency, such as plastic hangers, spices to grind, flashlights, and LED candles.

☐ Supporting children with sensory processing challenges may be complex. Some are highly sensitive to sensory stimulation while others have lower sensitivity. Children who crave more stimulation can grind herbs and spices with mortars and pestles to engage their sense of smell. Sand trays with natural Loose Parts help them feel the texture, coldness, and movement of the sand. Clay combined with wood sticks, shells, rocks, and other natural Loose Parts can satisfy their sense of touch. Children who are overly sensitive can try sand play with a brush or stick. Using gloves when manipulating clay may help them gain better control of the material.

☐ Be aware of overstimulation. For some children, watching flashing lights is a sensory delight; those same lights trigger seizures in other children. Consult with your care and education team (such as occupational therapist, speech therapist, physical therapist, and early childhood special education experts) and learn everything that you need to support each child.

☐ Make sure the Loose Parts are developmentally appropriate. Keep age, abilities, and skill in mind when designing a provocation. When children are still exploring with their mouths, make sure the activities you introduce are nontoxic and have pieces large enough not to present a choking hazard.

☐ The best place to promote children's curiosity and playfulness is nature itself. Children explore the variety of textures, colors, objects, forms, sounds, and smells of nature at their own pace and ability. Going on walks to feel the wind, sun, and rain engages children's sense of touch. Observe and notice what is pleasurable and what seems painful and adjust accordingly.

☐ Design indoor spaces with different textures. Soft cushions and blankets support children who experience challenges with hard surfaces. A balance of soft and hard surfaces and Loose Parts gives children choices.

☐ Have different working and playing opportunities in the ecosystem. Children can stand, or they can sit on sensory bouncy balls, pillows, blankets, or stools. Include a nook with a hammock, rocking chair, or swing for children to engage the vestibular system.

☐ Design spaces for messy experiences.

☐ Incorporate opportunities for movement both outside and inside to support children in exploring the sensations of touch.

☐ Lighting contributes to children's perceptions of the environment and their learning. Include natural light, table lamps, LED lights, and bright overhead lighting. Full-spectrum lightbulbs are more comfortable for children's eyes.

☐ Sit close together. The warmth of your presence is often enough to give easily stimulated children the physical touch they crave.

☐ Make physical interaction fun! Many Loose Parts provide much-needed physical touch without requiring too much of an emotional investment from your child.

☐ Sing songs with interactive hand motions or dance using scarves, dance ribbons, and other Loose Parts. Moving in unison, such as dancing, walking together, or singing songs with group hand motions stimulates the same feel-good endorphins as physical touch.

☐ Give children time to get used to a Loose Part. Sit next to the child and play with the Loose Part. When you notice hesitation to touch a Loose Part, offer verbal encouragement by describing how the object feels to the touch. Observe and respond as they allow for more contact and demonstrate comfort with touching an object on their own.

☐ For children who want to engage in play but have high reactivity to loud noise, consider redesigning the spaces to create protective areas where they can interact and play with Loose Parts without auditory disruption.

☐ Collect a variety of fabrics and papers that can be used as a background for the Loose Parts.

☐ Select Loose Parts that are quickly disinfected and cleaned for children in hospital settings.

2. Vision and Sight

☐ Select Loose Parts that do not have sharp edges and will not break.

☐ Set up Loose Parts for exploring lights and shadows.

☐ Provide Loose Parts that support children's observational skills—prisms, magnifying glasses of different shapes and sizes, and nonbreakable mirrors.

☐ Different textured surfaces can help children define the shape and form of the blocks.

☐ Include Loose Parts with contrasting colors, such as black circles on white backgrounds or white circles on black backgrounds.

☐ Children who are blind or partially sighted benefit from Loose Parts both large and small that offer textured surfaces. Light tables, overhead projectors, and flashlights can help them notice objects. Colorful acrylic containers in a variety of sizes are attractive and captivating.

☐ Be sure lighting is appropriate. Children need to read facial cues and expressions.

3. Hearing

☐ Deaf children and children who are hard of hearing need Loose Parts that vibrate. Drums, pots, pans, metal lids, wooden salad bowls, cans, and plastic bottles with gravel, small pebbles, and beads serve as shakers so children can participate in sing-alongs.

☐ Make the sound-producing and vibratory Loose Parts available to all children and do not single out the child who is deaf or hard of hearing.

☐ Ensure adequate lighting for children to see facial cues and read expressions.

☐ Include different types of brushes to support children's need for touch. Create baskets with sponges, loofahs, facial sponges, and washcloths.

☐ Introduce textured paper so children with diverse abilities can design, create, and explore. The sound the paper makes when folded can attract their attention.

☐ Provide small and large indoor sand trays and tables and hide precious stones or colorful glass beads to encourage children with diverse abilities to touch and search for them.

☐ Soft paint rollers can provide pressure point stimulation.

☐ Include surfaces that are multitextured or are in some other way pleasing and interesting to touch and see.

4. Motor Development

☐ Large Loose Parts encourage children to crawl and walk on different surfaces. Use rock tiles, bubble wrap, wood planks, cement blocks, carpet pieces, and large fabric swatches.

☐ Create opportunities for children to use their bodies as they explore the space, tools, materials, and Loose Parts.

☐ Give children control to move small and large items within their environment to challenge their kinesthetic abilities.

☐ Provide plenty of time outdoors so children engage in full-body movement and play.

☐ Support children in designing, creating, and constructing environments that challenge their bodies.

☐ Consider gross-motor and fine-motor skills as well as the proprioceptive and vestibular systems.

☐ Allow children to stand as they engage in fine-motor activities.

☐ Provide ribbons for dancing.

☐ Add low stools, tables, tree stumps (indoors and outdoors), and shelves children can use to come to a standing position.

☐ Use adaptive tools to facilitate engagement.

☐ Have children use a table easel if they need to work while sitting down.

☐ Incorporate bilateral play exploration—provide clothespins to connect and disconnect and blocks of different shapes and sizes that require the use of both hands.

☐ Add a basket of healthy snacks to encourage children to chew and crunch, which builds facial muscles.

☐ Encourage children to blow feathers of different sizes to strengthen facial muscle tone.

☐ Use silicone straws, tools, and wands of different sizes to blow bubbles.

☐ Incorporate trampolines and fitness balance balls to strengthen core muscles.

☐ Revisit your rules and make space for children to go up the slide.

☐ Use tubes and boxes of different sizes to create obstacle courses to build strength, endurance, and motor planning.

☐ Provide ladders that can be moved and placed at different heights to encourage climbing up and down. This targets both concentric movement (the lifting motion when the muscle shortens and its two connection points come close together that acts against the force of gravity and improves the muscle's ability to pull and lift) and eccentric movement (the length of the muscle increases as tension is produced, which facilitates the next muscle movement and provides elasticity).

☐ Provide clay for children to manipulate to improve the fine-motor skills needed to correctly grip a pencil or hold tools and utensils.

☐ Supply large Velcro dots for children to jump between and to move into different configurations to make the course more challenging.

5. Proprioceptive and Vestibular Systems

☐ Add heavy Loose Parts that can be pushed, pulled, and lifted—large and medium wooden spools to roll, tires to stack, large river rocks to move, and small tree stumps to pull in a wagon.

☐ Provide fabric pieces and wooden crates to make forts for hiding.

☐ Provide stepping-stones of various sizes for children to create jumping games.

☐ Offer large boat ropes for children to drag.

☐ Use wood pallets, large wood planks, straw bales, bicycle tires, bricks, and large tubes to create obstacle courses.

☐ Children can test how their bodies move by using Hula-Hoops or rolling the hoops on the ground using a stick.

☐ Blankets, pillows, and cushions may be used both indoors and outdoors.

☐ Children can explore movements by lining up carpet roll tubes and moving their bodies on top of them.

☐ Provide different sizes of tubes for children to push into clay or connect and disconnect. Add nuts and bolts to twist and screw.

☐ When engaging in vestibular activities, observe children for signs of over-stimulation and adjust input accordingly.

6. Critical Thinking and Executive Functions

☐ Incorporate a variety of textures to provoke interest and capture children's curiosity.

☐ Organize Loose Parts for accessibility and to promote children's autonomy. Organize the Loose Parts, tools, and materials so they are easily identified and accessed. Baskets facilitate moving the Loose Parts to different areas of the ecosystem.

☐ Observe and document children's interests and curate Loose Parts that will support them in further exploring their hypotheses. Infuse Loose Parts into the ecosystem to challenge complex thinking.

☐ Respond to children's interests by adding provocations and asking critical-thinking questions. Create opportunities for children, including children with diverse abilities, to explore and test their ideas. Adapt the process to support children's individual strengths. Formulate questions that help them think of multiple possibilities and solutions to a problem.

☐ Set the environment and schedule so that children can spend a considerable amount of time exploring and testing their ideas.

☐ Provide plenty of time for children to practice new skills until they develop a sense of mastery. This is particularly important for children with diverse abilities.

☐ Have more of the same type of Loose Parts, tools, and materials to increase exploration, rather than only a few of many types.

☐ Use visual organizational aids that remind children of daily routines.

☐ Plan and structure transition times and shifts in activities. Keeping transitions to a minimum is helpful.

☐ Provide opportunities for children to revisit their work by creating a space or system that allows the work to remain intact for at least a week.

☐ Schedule a weekly time to clean and organize the workspace.

7. Creativity

☐ Focus on children's strengths and create Loose Parts provocations that offer inspiration and challenge and support children with diverse abilities.

☐ Make Loose Parts available for long periods so children can explore them at their own pace.

☐ Design areas for accessibility so children with diverse abilities have access to all the shelves and areas where Loose Parts are stored.

☐ Give children with diverse abilities the opportunity to revisit an exploration as long as they need to make sense of it and test their creative spirit.

☐ Create documentation boards to make children's learning visible. Children with diverse abilities benefit from using the documentation to revisit and remember their creative projects.

☐ Keep to a predictable schedule to allow children with diverse abilities to explore their creativity within their common routines and rituals.

☐ Take photographs of children's transient art and display them around the classroom. Children appreciate seeing their work become part of the ecosystem.

General Considerations

☐ Observe children's reactions. A perplexed look or doing nothing may indicate a lack of understanding.

☐ Children use all their senses, and when one sense is not present, they will compensate by using other senses. Adding visual representations increases communication and helps children maneuver the ecosystem as they play with Loose Parts.

☐ Show real-life pictures when reading or talking about a topic; a photo of a block structure or visual documentation boards of children engaged in Loose Parts play can serve as an inspiration and strengthen understanding.

☐ Design spaces for collaborative Loose Parts play.

☐ Create opportunities for adult and peer modeling.

☐ Plan to offer children plenty of time to engage with the Loose Parts. Create a temporal space that gives children enough time to complete an activity.

☐ Evaluate the Loose Parts you will add to the ecosystem. Consider the affordances and the adaptations that will be necessary.

References

Abraira, Victoria E., and David D. Ginty. 2013. "The Sensory Neurons of Touch." *Neuron* 79, no. 4 (August 21): 618–39. https://doi.org/10.1016/j.neuron.2013.07.051.

Armstrong, Thomas. 1998. *Awakening Genius in the Classroom*. Alexandria, VA: ASCD.

ASCD (Association for Supervision and Curriculum Development). 2012. *Making the Case for Educating the Whole Child*. www.wholechildeducation.org/assets/content /mx-resources/WholeChild-MakingTheCase.pdf.

Bandura, Albert, ed. 1997. *Self-Efficacy in Changing Societies*. Cambridge: Cambridge University Press.

Beloglovsky, Miriam, and Michelle Grant-Groves. 2021. *Design in Mind: A Framework for Sparking Ideas, Collaboration, and Innovation in Early Education*. St. Paul, MN: Redleaf Press.

Booth, Sally, and Michele Claeys. 2010. "The Ross Model in Sweden." In *Educating the Whole Child for the Whole World*, edited by Marcelo M. Suarez-Orozco and Carolyn Sattin-Bajaj, 171–88. New York: New York University Press. https://doi.org/10.18574 /nyu/9780814741405.003.0014.

Booth, Tony, Mel Ainscow, and Denise Kingston. 2006. *Index for Inclusion: Developing Play, Learning and Participation in Early Years and Childcare*. Bristol, UK: Centre for Studies on Inclusive Education.

Bruner, Jerome. 2003. *Making Stories: Law, Literature, Life*. Cambridge, MA: Harvard University Press.

Campbell, Fiona Kumari. 2009. *Contours of Ableism: The Production of Disability and Abledness*. Basingstoke, UK: Palgrave Macmillan.

Carr, Margaret, and Wendy Lee. 2019. *Learning Stories in Practice*. London: Sage.

Chesworth, Liz. 2016. "A Funds of Knowledge Approach to Examining Play Interests: Listening to Children's and Parents' Perspectives." *International Journal of Early Years Education* 24, no. 3: 294–308. https://doi.org/10.1080/09669760.2016.1188370.

Crenshaw, Kimberlé. 1989. "Demarginalizing the Intersection of Race and Sex: A Black Feminist Critique of Antidiscrimination Doctrine, Feminist Theory and Antiracist Politics." *University of Chicago Legal Forum*, 1989, no. 1: 139–67.

Csikszentmihalyi, Mihaly. 2013. *Creativity: The Psychology of Discovery and Invention*. New York: Harper Perennial Modern Classics. Kindle.

De Vos, Gail, Merle Harris, and Celia Barker Lottridge. 1995. *Telling Tales: Storytelling in the Family*. Edmonton: University of Alberta Press.

Derman-Sparks, Louise, and Julie Olsen Edwards. 2020. *Anti-Bias Education for Young Children and Ourselves.* 2nd ed. Washington, DC: National Association for the Education of Young Children.

Division for Early Childhood of the Council for Exceptional Children. 2014. "DEC Recommended Practices in Early Intervention/Early Childhood Special Education 2014." www.dec-sped.org/Recommended-practices.

Edmiston, Brian. 2008. *Forming Ethical Identities in Early Childhood Play.* New York: Routledge. Kindle.

Erikson, Erik Homburger. 1977. *Toys and Reasons: Stages in the Ritualization of Experience.* New York: Norton.

Fisher, Anna V., Karrie E. Godwin, and Howard Seltman. 2014. "Visual Environment, Attention Allocation, and Learning in Young Children: When Too Much of a Good Thing May Be Bad." *Psychological Science* 25, no. 7 (July 1): 1362–70. https://doi .org/10.1177/0956797614533801.

Gardner, Howard. 1999. *Intelligence Reframed: Multiple Intelligences for the 21st Century.* New York: Basic Books.

González, Norma, Luis C. Moll, and Cathy Amanti, eds. 2005. *Funds of Knowledge: Theorizing Practices in Households, Communities, and Classrooms.* New York: Routledge.

Greenspan, Stanley I., Serena Wieder, and Robin Simons. 1998. *The Child with Special Needs: Encouraging Intellectual and Emotional Growth.* Reading, MA: Perseus Books. Kindle.

Hall, Kathy, Maura Cunneen, Denice Cunningham, Mary Horgan, Rosaleen Murphy, and Anna Ridgway. 2010. *Loris Malaguzzi and the Reggio Emilia Experience.* https://doi .org/10.5040/9781472541208.

Hannaford, Carla. 2005. *Smart Moves: Why Learning Is Not All in Your Head.* 2nd ed. Salt Lake City, UT: Great River Books.

Hanscom, Angela J. 2016. *Balanced and Barefoot: How Unrestricted Outdoor Play Makes for Strong, Confident, and Capable Children.* Oakland, CA: New Harbinger. Kindle.

Iheanacho, Franklin, and Anantha Ramana Vellipuram. 2019. "Physiology, Mechanoreceptors." *StatPearls* [internet]. Treasure Island, FL: StatPearls. Article last updated September 29, 2020. www.ncbi.nlm.nih.gov/books/NBK541068.

Isbell, Rebecca, and Shirley C. Raines. 2013. *Creativity and the Arts with Young Children.* 3rd ed. Belmont, CA: Wadsworth. Kindle.

Jensen, Eric. 2005. *Teaching with the Brain in Mind.* Alexandria, VA: Association for Supervision and Curriculum Development.

Johnson, Susan. "Teaching Our Children to Write, Read & Spell: Part 1." Waldorf Library. www.waldorflibrary.org/articles/1236-teaching-our-children-to-write-read-a-spell -part-1.

Kaufman, James C., and Robert. J. Sternberg, eds. 2019. *The Cambridge Handbook of Creativity.* 2nd ed. Cambridge: Cambridge University Press. Kindle.

Kaufman, Scott Barry, and Carolyn Gregoire. 2015. *Wired to Create: Unraveling the Mysteries of the Creative Mind.* New York: TarcherPerigee.

Kolb, Bryan, Allonna Harker, and Robbin Gibb. 2017. "Principles of Plasticity in the Developing Brain." *Developmental Medicine & Child Neurology* 59, no. 12 (December): 1218–23. https://doi.org/10.1111/dmcn.13546.

Landreth, Garry L. 2012. *Play Therapy: The Art of the Relationship*. 3rd ed. New York: Brunner-Routledge.

Libertus, Klaus, and Petra Hauf. 2017. "Editorial: Motor Skills and Their Foundational Role for Perceptual, Social, and Cognitive Development." *Frontiers in Psychology* 8. https://doi.org/10.3389/fpsyg.2017.00301.

Linder, Toni W. 1993. *Transdisciplinary Play-Based Assessment: A Functional Approach to Working with Young Children*. Rev. ed. Baltimore: Paul H. Brookes.

Luthar, Suniya S. 2003. *Resilience and Vulnerability: Adaptation in the Context of Childhood Adversities*. Cambridge: Cambridge University Press. Kindle.

Mayall, Berry. 2013. *A History of the Sociology of Childhood*. London: Institute of Education Press.

Montessori, Maria, and Barbara Barclay Carter. 2019. *The Secret of Childhood*. Eastford, CT: Martino Fine Books.

Morris, Robin, and Geoff Ward, eds. 2005. *The Cognitive Psychology of Planning*. New York: Psychology Press.

Muhammad, Gholdy. *Cultivating Genius: An Equity Framework for Culturally and Historically Responsive Literacy*. New York: Scholastic. Kindle.

National Scientific Council on the Developing Child. 2004. *Young Children Develop in an Environment of Relationships: Working Paper No. 1*. www.developingchild.harvard.edu/resources/wp1.

Nicholson, Simon. 1971. "How NOT to Cheat Children: The Theory of Loose Parts." *Landscape Architecture*, 62:30–34.

Oby, Emily R., Matthew D. Golub, Jay A. Hennig, Alan D. Degenhart, Elizabeth C. Tyler-Kabara, Byron M. Yu, Steven M. Chase, and Aaron P. Batista. 2019. "New Neural Activity Patterns Emerge with Long-Term Learning." *Proceedings of the National Academy of Sciences*, 116, no. 30: 15210–15. https://doi.org/10.1073/pnas.1820296116.

Paley, Vivian Gussin. 1990. *The Boy Who Would Be a Helicopter*. Cambridge, MA: Harvard University Press.

Panksepp, Jaak. 2014. *Affective Neuroscience: The Foundations of Human and Animal Emotions*. Oxford: Oxford University Press.

Pink, Daniel H. 2009. *Drive: The Surprising Truth about What Motivates Us*. New York: Riverhead Books.

Play and Playground Encyclopedia. 2016. S.v. "Sara Smilansky." June 27. www.pgpedia.com/s/sara-smilansky.

Pretti-Frontczak, Kristie, and Diane Bricker. 2004. *An Activity-Based Approach to Early Intervention*. 3rd ed. Baltimore MD: Paul H. Brookes.

Proske, Uwe, and Simon C. Gandevia. 2016. "Proprioception: The Sense Within." *Scientist* 30, no. 9 (September 1). https://research.monash.edu/en/publications/proprioception-the-sense-within.

Quinn, Joanne, and Kenneth H. Rubin. 2018."The Play of Handicapped Children." In *Selected Introductory Notes on Child's Play as Developmental and Applied. Children's Play*, edited by Thomas D. Yawkey, 1–7. https://doi.org/10.4324/9781315099071-1.

Ritchhart, Ron, Mark Church, and Karin Morrison. 2011. *Making Thinking Visible: How to Promote Engagement, Understanding, and Independence for All Learners.* San Francisco: Jossey-Bass. Kindle.

Ritchhart, Ron, Terri Turner, and Linor Hadar. 2009. "Uncovering Students' Thinking about Thinking Using Concept Maps." *Metacognition and Learning* 4, no. 2 (January 31): 145–59. https://doi.org/10.1007/s11409-009-9040-x.

Rogers, Carl R. 1980. *A Way of Being.* New York: Houghton Mifflin.

Scruton, Roger. 2009. *Beauty.* New York: Oxford University Press.

Seefeldt, Carol. 1995. "Art—A Serious Work." *Young Children* 50, no. 3 (March): 39–45.

Silvia, Paul. J. 2006. *Exploring the Psychology of Interest.* New York: Oxford University Press.

Singer, Judy. 2017. *Neurodiversity: The Birth of an Idea.* Self-published.

Slade, Sean. 2015. "The Whole Child Initiative." *Promoting Health and Academic Success.* https://doi.org/10.5040/9781492596936.ch-004.

Sternberg, Robert J., and James C. Kaufman. 2018. *The Nature of Human Creativity.* New York: Cambridge University Press.

Torrance, E. Paul. 1993a. "Understanding Creativity: Where to Start?" *Psychological Inquiry,* 4, no. 3: 229–32. https://doi.org/10.1207/s15327965pli0403_17.

———. 1993b. "The Beyonders in a Thirty-Year Longitudinal Study of Creative Achievement." *Roeper Review* 15, no. 3 (February): 131–35. https://doi.org/10.1080/02783199309553486.

Turner, Mark. 1998. *The Literary Mind: The Origins of Thought and Language.* New York: Oxford University Press.

Vandenhole, Wouter, Gamze Erdem Türkelli, and Sara Lembrechts. 2019. "The Committee on the Rights of the Child." In *Children's Rights: A Commentary on the Convention on the Rights of the Child and Its Protocols,* 404–8, Paragraph 6 (e). Northampton, MA: Edward Elgar. https://doi.org/10.4337/9781786433138.00053.

U.S. Department of Health and Human Services. 2018. "How Do We Hear?" National Institute on Deafness and Other Communication Disorders. www.nidcd.nih.gov/health/how-do-we-hear.

University of Pittsburgh. 2019. "How the Brain Changes When Mastering a New Skill." *ScienceDaily.* June 10. www.sciencedaily.com/releases/2019/06/190610151934.htm.

University of Washington. 2001. "Brains of Deaf People Rewire to 'Hear' Music." *ScienceDaily,* November 28. www.sciencedaily.com/releases/2001/11/011128035455.htm.

Vélez-Ibáñez, Carlos G., and James B. Greenberg. 1992. "Formation and Transformation of Funds of Knowledge among U.S.-Mexican Households." *Anthropology & Education Quarterly* 23, no. 4 (December): 313–35. www.jstor.org/stable/3195869.

Venetsanou, Fotini, and Antonis Kambas. 2009. "Environmental Factors Affecting Preschoolers' Motor Development." *Early Childhood Education Journal* 37, no. 4: 319–27. https://doi.org/10.1007/s10643-009-0350-z.

Vygotsky, L. S., and Michael Cole. 1978. *Mind in Society: The Development of Higher Psychological Processes.* Cambridge: Harvard University Press.

Woodruff, C. Chad. 2018. "Reflections of Others and of Self: The Mirror Neuron System's Relationship to Empathy." In *The Neuroscience of Empathy, Compassion, and Self-Compassion,* edited by Larry Stevens and C. Chad Woodruff, 157–87. Cambridge, MA: Academic Press. https://doi.org/10.1016/b978-0-12-809837-0.00006-4.